Life Is How YOU Look At It

Nancy Loss

Edited by: Phyllis Stallard

WestBow
PRESS

A DIVISION OF THOMAS NELSON

Scripture taken from the New King James Version ®. Copyright © 1982 Thomas Nelson Inc. Used by permission. All rights reserved.

Cover Design by Robert Scalzo, Striking Poses Portrait Studio
Nancy Loss' Portrait Photographed by Robert Scalzo
Dog "Prince" Photographed by Robert Scalzo
Back Cover Vase/Roses Photographed by Robert Scalzo
Portrait of "Prince" used with permission of Jan Symon

*** With special thanks to Prince for handsomely appearing on my front cover; as he not only sat patiently for his picture, but also reflected humorously how it is possible to have one of "such royalty" appear right along with me! (And, kudos as well to his owner, Jan Symon, for blissfully letting me borrow him and so timely fitting in his photo shoot.)

*** A portion of the proceeds from the sale of this book will be donated to Habitat for Humanity, whose gifted talents allow others to exist amidst true dignity and treasured peace.

WestBow Press books may be ordered through booksellers or by contacting:

WestBow Press
A Division of Thomas Nelson
1663 Liberty Drive
Bloomington, IN 47403
www.westbowpress.com
1-(866) 928-1240

ISBN: 978-1-4497-4033-7 (hc)
ISBN: 978-1-4497-4034-4 (sc)
ISBN: 978-1-4497-4035-1 (e)

Library of Congress Control Number: 2012902526

Printed in the United States of America

WestBow Press rev. date: 09/06/2012

Table of Contents

Dedication ix

Preface..xi

Acknowledgements..xiii

Who Are You? 1

The Power of Prayer—When Rainbows Became Real Again............15

Always Cherish Your "I Love You's" 25

The Tapestry of Me 27

Do You Have a "Susie" Too? 29

When Life Appears Too Big, My Friend 35

A Lesson in High School Humility..51

Dare to Make a Difference by "Leaning In With Love" 59

When Life Sends Us What We're Lacking 79

How "Meister" Saved Christmas 85

Taking Time Out for Guaranteed Giggles 97

My Saving Grace Grandpa 107

The Gifts of "My Grandmas" 115

The Year I Lost My Smile...123

A Blessing from the Bible 127

From Teddy Bears to Answered Prayers 129

How Jerri "Did It Her Way"...145

The Magic of "My Michael's" 151

The Magic of My Michael's Part II 159

The Poem That Wouldn't Leave Me Alone 165

From "Rindercella" to Reality..171

From "Rindercella" to Reality—and the Rainbows in Between!.....179

"What Are You Willing to Give Up to Achieve Your Dream?".......185

Reaching for Rainbows...197

My Life Is How You Look At It Ending 199

My "Life Is How You Look At It" Homestretch 211

The "Special Three" Who Were Meant to Be.................267

A Word to Readers 273

My Hardest Life Lesson For Last...................................277

About the Author 289

Notes and Nuggets...291

Dedication

This book is dedicated to everyone who ever dared to dream. Therefore, once manifesting the miracle of these pages into print I shall like to share that my stories aren't always in order by timeline, but instead by their "tapestry threads." After all, we are all "survivors" of something, making life less about looking backwards and more about learning to heal. (Moreover, some of my story's grammar may truly not be perfect, as portrayed from the timely "age that I was.") So in the end, I hope that each of you will ponder your own chosen purpose, while *Life Is How YOU Look At It* leaves me a legacy of which to be proud!

Enjoy!

In Peace and Prayers,

Love, Nancy

Preface

In the early 2000's, I found myself alone at home and reflecting upon losing three so-loved people in just four so-short years. At this point, I negatively asked aloud to God "Why me?" to which He instantly replied "No, Why NOT you, *Life Is How YOU Look At It, Missy.*" And, since never having answered me before, this awakening thought process changed both my grief-filled doldrums and genuine destiny; allowing me to spiritually harvest also this sacredly written work.

Acknowledgements

With special thanks to my two daughters, who over time showed me that "Single Parenting" is not always a burden, but a chance to get real with our gifts. Michelle and Bethany, how proud I am to watch both of you strive towards your goals along with others that make you smile. And, to my intuitive Grandparents and Guardian Angels who believed in me, even before I believed in myself. I would also like to praise those cherished authors and creative experts whose input within (just when I really needed to learn things!) led to a place of higher peace. To Phyllis Stallard, Donna Crow and Beth MacSwan for your faithful editing, computer and copying finesse; I will be forever grateful for the support that you've become. Yet, most important is my gratitude to God for blessing me with "true family" and tender friendships, amidst teaching me that no matter how AWFUL my life gets I have the choice to let go with love.

Who Are You?

Take a moment to think about your birth name. Do you like the way it sounds? Did you ever curiously ask why your parents blessed (or cursed) you with it? Are there positive memories associated with its meaning? Have you spent any time researching the origin of your name in a baby book or on the Internet—to remind yourself just how special you are, while shedding more light on the subject? Would you consider changing your "had-to-have" name to one you would feel more in harmony with?

HOW IT ALL BEGAN: IN SEARCH OF MYSELF AMIDST "MEMOIRS OF MISSY"

I was born in November 1963, a few days before J.F.K. was assassinated, as a preemie struggling to survive. As tradition would have it, my parents named me after my aunt and I began my little life as Nancy Wyona Loss. Yet my Poppy always thought differently. To him, I would forever be "Missy." And, from the get-go, my aspiring grandfather was there to watch me grow! Each day, he'd be perched alongside my incubator until my lungs would be mature enough to leave hospital life behind for a busy home, and my trying-at-times big brother. So, even as I traded a "routine of true serenity" for times of sibling rivalry, Poppy was sure to keep me safe. Since he also had tons of spoiling to catch up on, he would eternally rock me to sleep, snuggled next to his calming heartbeat, especially as Mom was still preparing my supper! Moreover, my Grandfather knew it was no fluke that his tiny, miracle-of-a-granddaughter had remained on this much-needed earth. While I continued to sprout, Poppy would often say that I was born "gifted" and that God had a special purpose for me. And, for as long as I can remember, he always carried within his very weathered wallet a tiny newspaper clipping (a part of which appears below) to regularly remind him of me, his surely "heaven-sent Missy."

SKETCHES

" . . . sweet lips, soft lines upon her face . . . do more than words can state . . . she is an angel sent from God . . . so small and yet so great . . ."

~ Ben Burroughs

Although it would take me several years to "connect the clues" that I'd been uniquely chosen, I can honestly say that this somewhat uphill challenge has been well worth the insightful trip! Yet, like a five-year-old child playing dominoes with Poppy amidst resting my chin upon the tabletop, I had totally forgotten into semi-adulthood that sometimes life's pathways don't flow in a straight line, but may purposely zig-zag along the way. More importantly, I learned that by immersing head-first into my long-lost memoirs I was not only helping my readers but emotionally healing myself.

Looking back previously, there was very little I remembered about my background, while the "sketches" of my own retained memories seemed too painful at times to re-live. Positively though, there were some things I knew for sure! Foremost, as a small child, my father had been in the right place at the right time on two separate occasions. See, once to unconditionally give me life, the other to unexpectedly save my life. As the preschool story goes, once I magically made the transition from "touch-and-go" to thriving, it seems that my feisty older brother liked me more as a piggy bank than a person. It was now as a year-older toddler that he fed me a shiny penny that got stuck in my little throat. While my nurse-of-a-mom tried so diligently to dislodge it, I began to turn "blue" at the hands of this troublesome coin. But, as fate would have it, my never-called-in-sick father would be feeling under the weather that morning. Here, Dad's long middle finger made the difference in my plight, while successfully allowing his petite daughter to again stay put on this planet!

Months down the road, my younger sister appeared, making me the middle child (for now) amongst us Three Musketeers. Yet throughout all the growth spurts and giggles, I was endlessly teased by this twosome about my "goofy" middle name. As luck would have it also, I can still recall being around the age of seven when I curiously asked Poppy about why they'd chosen the name "Wyona"—while never letting on myself how much I hated what they had labeled me with! It was here that my grandfather's truthful response would make this embarrassing-laden issue so much easier to live with. Next, I learned how I'd not only been bestowed the name of a beautiful Indian woman, but also remained a long-term tribute to my Grammie's warm-fuzzy best friend.

Several years later, I would uncover even more of an enlightening answer to my negative-at-times name situation. Once beginning my freshman year at college, I found myself entering the campus library with no specific purpose but to scout out the place. Suddenly, I was overcome by a "spiritual sensation" to browse a certain section of beckoning books. Upon reaching the area I'd been "intuitively guided" to graze, my left hand instantly grasped an old hardcover on the insights of Indian Heritage. To my amazement, I discovered a detailed dictionary of ethnic names, including my own explained on well-worn paper. It was here, as I read the word "Wyona" that the scattered pieces of my lost patchwork began to slowly land into place. Finally, I learned that my goofy middle name meant genuinely "first-born daughter," which Aunt Nan and I both were! Now, I couldn't help but wonder, when coupled with my first name "Nancy" which means "gracious gift of God," could it be that my heads-up Grandparents had actually prepared their shy Missy to practice "real angelhood" right here on this Earth? Yet, no one would have a harder time accepting this agenda than I would. To add to my sudden dilemma, amidst discovering several decades of "comfort-quilt coincidences" in the design of my checkerboard past, how could I not share these once-suppressed details with the world? So, about twelve years ago, the apparent struggle began between staying on the straight and narrow as a single mom trying to make it, or surrendering the mundane of materialism to seriously make a name for myself.

Who Are You?—Part II

Meanwhile, I knew there was much about my list of names through the years that had made lasting imprints upon my identity. To those around me I have been called "Nanny," "Nanner," "Pretty" and "Poongle" (and laughably "Eddie Munster" after an extremely bad haircut, amongst other less-positives to never put into print), but always felt deep inside that something was missing. About this time too, a little "neighborhood angel" would appreciatively allow my aura to slip into something more comfortable. While her preacher-of-a-father strictly forbid her to call any adult by their first name (and pronouncing my then-married name was nearly next to impossible) we sweetly settled upon "Miss Nancy"—a seemingly simple combination of both my parent's daughterly desires and my Poppy's destiny for me! Since then, as my life-altering purpose has begun largely to prosper, I have added three more names to the list of my legacy. Due to my deep-seeded quest to acquire various things in my favorite color, I have been dubbed "The Queen of Purple," by a genuine sweetheart as he presented me one Valentine's Day with a stunning, grape-shaded Lava Lamp! While also believing in my motto "if it's purple then someday I'll own it," even I was beyond shocked to learn from a soul-touching stranger on the street the true meaning behind my set-in-stone thinking! See, while casually discussing the subject of amethyst rocks while frostily standing on a store's snow-crusted sidewalk, this knowledgeable person next informed me how our kindred favorite color isn't visible in regular light, but only in violet-like pigment. That is, he explained further, unless he "took a rainbow-filled spectrum and purposely combined the separate ends of red and blue into a sacred circle," allowing for the soothing shade of purple (which symbolizes Enlightenment!) to be especially produced. Moreover, this unexpected meeting of the minds was a real inspiration to me to continue along with my much-cherished task. Then, once all was said and done, this wind-blown man presented to me from the depths of his winter coat pocket a large cut of Amethyst stone that even now as I continue to meditate, helps to keep my concentration on course. Over the years too, I've also been appreciated for being a "Leopard Lovin' Lady" as reflected in a stylish array of animal print accessories—from slippers to scarves, and bed sheets to bathing suits. Where even today in my travels, people will stop and share their "I saw something leopard and thought of you" stories, while making me humorously also so easy to buy for!

Foremost though, my favorite nickname story has deeply touched my heart (while also altering some of the names herein for their protection of privacy). About seven years ago, I befriended an awesome single mom I'll simply call "Laurel." In the midst of both our casual and colorful discussions, she also shared the fact of being a successful cancer survivor. Her life appeared on the upswing now, with the worst of her battle-scars seemingly behind her, as evidenced by a flowing head of long, red hair framing a smile that spoke volumes! Remarkably too, Laurel was becoming a first-time bride next spring, complete with a faithful father figure for her nine-year-old son to savor. Yet, her long-term plan for happiness was abruptly halted when it was discovered that her cancer had returned. This time, it wreaked havoc upon her once healthy lymph nodes, allowing her non-suspecting doctors to approximate less than a year to live. Meanwhile, something drastically different developed. Laurel became determined to make her final months count, by not focusing on all she might miss out on; but by freely celebrating the miracles contained within the precious present! And, as the days wore on, she appeared so angelic. Due to a stream of radiation treatments, her mane-like tresses had been replaced by a much shorter cut that was thickly sprayed to both stick up and look stylish. While forever true to her non-stop spirit, this trendier look was nothing more than a mix of spontaneous and sporty, while never to be squashed behind a not-for-her bandana. At this challenging countdown, it was so much easier to capture the beauty in her tell-tale eyes, as no longer clouded by the thickness of long hair once covering the contours of her cheeks. Above all, she exuded a renewed freshness and contagious inner peace, amidst a real trooper readiness to accept her approaching fate. It was here that I could only hope to handle the "winding down of my own fragile hourglass" with such front-line finesse—should I too find myself with only months to live, children to care for and lots of dreams derailed. Luckily, this gut-wrenching moment was THE wake-up call I needed to begin my metamorphosis into the woman I was born to be! Besides (as my intuition whispered), who says these situations will always happen to someone else? Then, suddenly from this mind-blowing thought arose childhood flickers of being born on Mickey Mouse's birthday, dragging around a doll named "Susie", carefully collecting Cinderella memorabilia and forever-honoring the sight of recurrent "rainbow messages" in my once tourist-swamped hometown. Yet, these precious tapestry threads were not much to go on to manifest also (as Poppy believed) that pre-conceived mission of me. Likewise, I learned that the huge holes in my history would miraculously come to light each time that I chose to lapse into "Missy mode," after being mystically coaxed while meditating to cherish my own special name. Insightfully too, I knew I was entering a whole new dimension in life, and by simply letting those "scattered dominoes" just fall as they please, God would send me whomever I would need to succeed!

Shortly thereafter, I remember feeling twinges of sadness as Laurel's printed obituary appeared in the pages of our local newspaper. At the same time, I was filled with an overwhelming burst of gratefulness that the brave beacon she'd become had blessed my path to begin with. Now, can you guess what three *Life Is How YOU Look At It* lessons were left behind by Laurel, for me to never forget? First, life is far too short to worry about a supposed "bad hair day," as many people would give anything to even have some hair to stress about! Second, I've witnessed how we all have the skills to be an inspiration to others regardless of accessories or income, since it is what's stored inside each of us that truly matters the most. Lastly, if you are repeatedly being interrupted with thoughts of people you need to call or catch up with, these are never coincidences but "angelic nudges" to help keep your authentic priorities in place.

Who Are You?—Part III

A few weeks after Laurel's last breath, I found myself reflecting upon her non-stop charisma. At the same time, I was comfortably reclined at a new hairstylist's sink, as she massaged some much-needed conditioner into my thirsty scalp. Once seated at "Tammy's" workstation, our conversation revolved around what to do about my outdated look. Next, she openly suggested that I replace my longer locks with something more original. Then, to better prove her point, she whisked my chair around to view a wall-sized photo while also in the moment exclaiming: "That model's striking haircut was made just for you!" To my surprise, I now sat face-to-face with none other than Laurel's trademark short hairstyle! Needless to say, it only took a few seconds to make up my mind and my once heavy hair fell to the floor in a hurry. Then, as my ten-years-younger makeover became more apparent in the mirror, I was filled with a complete understanding of my Grammie's gracious need to name me after her unique girlfriend! Moreover, I left the salon a changed woman that Friday, amidst paying tribute to a fabulous lady whose memory could live on in my looks. Yet this was only the beginning of my enlightenment towards the truth!

Upon returning the next morning to my emergency room desk, I would never have imagined the favorable response this daring haircut would create amongst my day-to-day coworkers. Here, Dr. Perry Spavento began to call me "Spike," a laugh-out-loud nickname that has since stuck like major glue, while leaving longtime Miss Nancy somewhere in the dust. Inside too, I secretly savored how this spontaneous new look had so little to do with exposing my own femininity, and was more about expressing my love for a free-spirited female too fearless to forget! About the same time, another treasured physician let me in on a little secret. After years of him faithfully watching me work, he enlightened me how

I was aglow with "Angelic Tendencies," incredibly gifted to guide others with illuminating visions, laughter and love; while also finally giving a name to that undeniable warmth I'd always experienced. Though, this pleasurable sensation was something that I am sure I inherited from my Poppy, as I can still remember being awestruck by the sheer beauty of his healing purpose, one of which he'd always encouraged me to pursue. Besides, as some of my family believed, I wasn't born "bad" (as repeatedly told through the years) but spiritually blessed, a sacred talent this "teacher" noted was not to be taken lightly. Now, at this shocking moment, I foremost felt that "growing into my giftedness" involved creating some written wisdom for others like me in search of themselves! Next, the awakening survivor I am, appealed to the spirit world to allow me more subjects to make sense of it all. Lastly, I promised the Lord that if I too, like Laurel, should be "borrowed as a beacon" I would not let Him down—amidst being truly caught off guard by the love that came full circle, as I proceeded onward and upward with this worthwhile cause.

*** Now for my readers, please stop and surmise:

Throughout the years, what inspirational song, saying or sonnet best describes your personal perception of yourself today? Does this overall thought process allow only your true positives to prevail?

*** My most treasured "mirror" along these lines is the blessed lived-and-learned insight of *I'm a Survivor.*

The Power of Prayer—When Rainbows Became Real Again

Although I've always been intuitive, I've gratefully learned throughout the last several years just how much I can rely on this gift to spiritually show me the way. Fact was, about eight years ago I was struggling for peaceful solutions to an overwhelming spectrum of issues in my life from faith, to friends to finances. I was also busy "faking fulfillment," by forever-smiling to the outside world. Yet, on the inside was an undeniable emptiness that I continued to ignore, until stuffing it within no longer worked. Each day I felt as stifled as "an experimental laboratory rat" in someone else's structured maze. Though one thing I knew for sure, it was easier to stay immersed in other people's ordeals then to embark upon the healing of my own inner heartaches. While meditating also, the universe was sending me a clear-cut message. Here, I could visualize a rapidly approaching fork in the road along my fact-finding journey I have now nicknamed "from victim to Victorious." Next, I was warmly informed that if I chose to take on the right path, I could easily cannonball into the challenge of change, cease controlling everything's outcome, and continue to celebrate my clairvoyance, while also enjoying the new-found energy that the excitement of the unknown provided. On the other hand, if I remained stuck in a false sense of security by forever "clinging by my fingernails" to the cliffs of my comfort zone, I would never unleash the freedom to fly! In the end, I opted to make the right (and only) decision, while assuming full responsibility head-on for my own happiness.

My lessons have been hard, but I invite you to celebrate them with me. When looking back now, there were times when I felt like I was truly traveling through the "car wash of chaos" with the convertible top down. After all, we each know how lousy it feels to wind up with unexpected soap in our eyes, as it not only stings, but then clouds our vision of reality. Yet, with every negative obstacle emerged a positive growth spurt. And, by fatefully opening the doors on my forgotten past, I've forever added one brick at a time to the precious faith-filled foundation of me. Wondrously also, I have learned to watch for "windows" when seeking out spiritual solutions to all of my situations. Here too, amidst an ever-so-soothing combination of clarity and comfort, I've consciously learned to soak up the view while savoring every

moment for the special gift that it is. Then, by embarking
to expose the underlying meaning of each person, place
or possession that has purposely crossed my path, I have
playfully, yet at times painfully, managed to uncover the
once missing "puzzle pieces" of my own precious-to-me past.
Even more enlightening though, I delightfully discovered
that the makings of divine miracles aren't always meant for
everyone else!

At this point, I also found myself haunted by some
harsh pre-teen memories that I needed to delve into deeper
before being able to release them. So, faithfully as always, I
entrusted my mixed feelings to my wonderful male friend,
Michael, where throughout these times of me "spiritually
being summoned" his show of support remains unmatched.
In this case as well, his ingrained knack for listening intently
and ever-knowing just what to say was again right on
target. Somehow too, as I relentlessly spilled my previously
suppressed "rat in a maze" flashbacks, he silently absorbed my
words then softly responded: "When you turn on the lights
Honey, the rats will scatter." You see, he'd already traveled
down this thought-provoking road, ugly rats and all! Yet,
happily here, the more I faced my irrational fears the quicker
they seemed to dissipate, while unveiling many unforeseen
pathways that truly became mine-for-the-mention. Now,
I am sure that it is perfectly proper to shed those people,

places and possessions that no longer serve us in a healthy way. This assertive step towards "lighter living" leaves others wearing the weight of their own emotional baggage, while rightfully releasing our need of regularly rescuing them. I've also learned to rely on my own "personal parachute" for optimal support, while successfully knowing it will always open safely, whenever I continue to nurture my soul first and foremost. But, during these tougher years too, I truly sustained my sanity amidst religiously practicing the concept of "Serenity through Surrender." Incredibly, by repeatedly releasing all my concerns into God's trustworthy hands, I rediscovered that He would always take care of the rest as long as I kept my priorities straight . . .

The Power of Prayer—Part II

It was late January 1994. While I was busy trying out some relatively new "stress squishing skills," my sister Becky's strength reserves were being rigorously tested from several directions also. In the early 1990's, she had married and moved cross-country to California to love, honor and cherish her new husband, while he continued his commitment to the U.S. Government. Next, they became the proud parents of little "Isabella Angelina" who was about a year old when Becky got pregnant again. Almost instantly, I learned to appreciate my now-absentee sister and "new aunt" status amidst our long distance updates—with the added bonus of enjoying little Izzy's giggle-filled gibberish!

Yet, during this time, Becky and I would have more in common than just our sisterly bond. For both of us, our second pregnancies would be much tougher on our bodies. Unexpectedly also, as these All-American parents eagerly anticipated the "routine results" of a prenatal sonogram, the technician's findings were alarmingly abnormal. Here, this ultrasound detected a mass thought to be an enlarging pelvic tumor residing along with their baby. Before my sister knew what was happening, she was signing consent forms for emergency surgery while sadly needing to abort their baby-to-be. Her doctors would be removing both the unwelcome growth and her expanding uterus, while hoping to spare Becky's own precious life should this untimely tumor prove cancerous. With this swift change in circumstances, our single mom boarded upon the next flight she could schedule out to California, while needing to say goodbye to her less-than-flexible workplace in order to put her family's needs first. Moreover, I was torn too, by not being able to be at Becky's side. Still, I wholeheartedly pledged some long-distance love amid some last-ditch hopes that she'd somehow manage to pull through this.

On Becky's surgery day, I found myself busily folding some laundry throughout this bleak winter morning at home. And, while purposely trying to distract my train of thought from my younger "sibling's date with fate," it suddenly occurred to me that my only sister's outcome was surely out of my own hands. Then, routinely as always, I entered my daughter Bethany's bedroom and placed a pile of clean laundry upon the comforts of her bed. Where, at this very "mundane minute," I was uniquely overcome by an uncontrollable urge to pray! Funny, after my first divorce I'd felt far less than a fellow Catholic, as my once-firmer religious beliefs had seemingly slipped by the wayside. While also assuming that God's steadfast love radiated more towards those with non-scarred track records, I rarely attended mass anymore. Next, amidst sobs of sadness, I dropped to my knees and closed my eyes in prayer. I asked God to provide my sister and her husband His powerful strength to successfully see through this. I also wished for Him to spare from harm, our precious unborn baby she was carrying as well. Then suddenly, the soothing presence of bright sunlight flickered through Bethany's window and warmed my tear-streaked face! While I pensively buried my head in my hands, I could not control the seemingly endless drips of emotion that ever-so-gently soaked my daughter's pink pillow. Next, I truly thanked God for sharing the gift of His sunshine with me. At this moment of gripping uncertainty, I asked Him also to please "send me a sign" that my only sister would be ok. As I opened my swollen eyes after that heartfelt prayer, I was honestly amazed! Dancing amongst the soft sunbeams that filtered through Bethany's half-open blinds was a huge, sparkling rainbow illuminating up her whole room! I was breathless as I marveled at its beauty. At this heartwarming time, tears again covered my cheeks as I knew in an instant that God had heard my prayer. He'd remarkably assured me too, that Becky and her sweet baby were safely held within His Hands! To my surprise, since this stressful situation seemed so much bigger than I was, surrendering came easy. And, once accomplished, a "calm sense of peacefulness" enveloped my awakening heart, an awesome feeling I've grown to give thanks for, whether one-on-one with God or openly interacting with others who touch me deeply. Seconds later, our mom called to confirm what the Lord had already enlightened me with. Becky had safely "held her own" throughout the surgery and her littlest angel was still housed within her womb! That "apparent tumor" was a twisted cyst that had fallen off from her ovary, awkwardly landing in an unusual area, and therefore labeled as an abnormal mass. From this point on, our tiny wonder, who had yet to make her Earthly entrance, struggled to maintain many months of premature contractions. Meanwhile, my once-busy sister became no stranger to bed rest. Then, down the road, when her doctors felt her baby's organs were strong enough to sustain the ways of the outside world, Becky finally delivered a dainty girl named "Gina." At this treasured time, she always appeared "petite, happy and beyond bald." Gratefully too, Gina and I will eternally share a *Life Is How YOU Look At It* cherished connection, based on the long-shot survivors we both are! Today, she still remains precious, as a beautiful reminder that God has showered us with her sweet presence. Lastly, my sister Becky and I added another facet to the "Specialness of our Sisterhood." See, we'd both been blessed with two baby girls each, mine were born in July and March on the sixth of the month, while hers appeared in January and June on the twelfth of those months. Wondrously, I will always savor the magic of these miracles, as I am still awestruck by the appearance of "real rainbows" when all-out asking for guidance from God. This insightful experience especially holds true on those emotionally charged issues, where the illuminating answers aren't always crystal clear, but in the end "arrive" well-worth the wait!

Baby Gina
1 ½ years old

Always Cherish Your "I Love You's"

As my niece Gina grew, she would spend time with her "favorite" Aunt Nanny, while Mommy and Izzy would have a field day at the mall. And, while my own girls were at school, we would always watch a cartoon video and cook a fresh batch of macaroni and cheese to soothe our starving stomachs. On one such afternoon, I was preparing our lunch and washing some dishes as Gina quietly amused herself with a coloring book by my feet. But, somewhere between all the suds and the stirring, I had somehow not noticed the new picture she'd scribbled all over my freshly painted cupboards! You see, only weeks earlier I'd remodeled my kitchen with clusters of yellow daisies wrapped in ribbons of checkerboard blue. Though, to my regret, one of these newly touched-up cabinets was now largely covered in real streaks of chocolate brown crayon. Meanwhile, I let out a groan while not knowing who I was more peeved at, this tiny girl for her "masterpiece" or me for not watching my niece. Yet, as almost two-year-old Gina awaited my next move, it dawned on me just how silly this whole situation was. After all, I (as the only adult in the room!) had the choice to make light of it. That's when I bent down to caress her blonde hair and tickle the base of her chin. Then, as my niece's stunned expression was replaced by a sweet smile, I told her softly: "It's ok Gina, Aunt Nanny still loves you." To which she instantly fired back in her squeaky, toddler voice "I love you too, DAMN IT!" So even today, as those ugly streaks of brown crayon still reappear on that cupboard no matter how many times I paint over them, I really have learned to cherish my "I Love You's" however they may come!

The Tapestry of Me

The tapestry threads of yesteryear mixed with "Angels on Earth" from today connect the patchwork for my own "Comfort quilt wrapped in Love" as the gift of God's light leads the way. As each and every time I surrender my struggles, I count on the universe to answer me back- while sometimes receiving responses only I understand, I'm sent "special signs" that I'm on the right track!

*God's guidance
*Red Roses
*Family and friends
*Miracles
*Music and Dance
*Warm-fuzzies
*Lipstick/lotions
*Sunshine and stars
*Soft pajamas
*Prayers and poems

*Holidays
*Dolls
*Butterflies
*Rain/Nature
*Books
*Recipes
*Love
*Toilet paper (honest!)
*Cinderella
*Doctors

*Leopard print fabric

*Angels and fate

*Children

*Anything purple

*Rainbows

*Kisses and hugs

*Pillows/Blankets

*The "Grinch"

*Rocking chairs

*Teachers

You are cordially invited to wallow in the wonders of magical memories, while quietly reflecting upon your own "lucky charms." From forgotten hobbies and favorite places, to fashion statements and familiar faces- it is never too late to celebrate life through the excited eyes of an eight-year-old!

Do You Have a "Susie" Too?

While cleaning one night I found my old baby doll,
Wedged up in the closet between clean sheets and the wall.
A birthday gift from my favorite Aunt Nan
At rest peacefully now up in heaven,
Carried her 'round by her now-knotted hair
From the time I was young, till age seven.
Picking "Susie" up, I noticed
That she needed to be hugged.
She was kind of dusty,
And she needed to be loved!
Running my fingers through her messy blonde hair,
I held her closely up to my chest.
Half-snuggling and rocking her gently,
How she just loved to be caressed!
Her eyes how they've dimmed
From the once brightest blue,
Ever keeping the secrets
Only she and I knew.

Her cherry lips had faded
Into the color of dusty rose,
With traces of lipstick "makeovers"
Under her wrinkled up nose.
Still looking the same to me
Were her tiny perfect ears-
Always ready to listen,
Soothing away my biggest fears!
Her yellow dress was bright and sunny
Against her silky skin so fair,
And we both still shared our passion
For frilly underwear!
I brought her back up to my face
And hugged her to my cheek,
With her chest now right up, close to mine-
Our hearts never skipped a beat.
I pulled her string but she talks no more
As she guides me only in spirit,
Her little voice remains part of me,
When I go "within" I still hear it.
I whispered to her that I'd missed her,
And was happy she'd found her way home.
Like angels, she and Aunt Nan watch over me-
So I will never feel totally alone.
She told me it's time to "play again"

Within my reach are all my desires,
Reminding me how much the Girl Scouts in us loved-
Fishing trips, s'mores and bon-fires.
Continuing our journey back in time,
I rode my bike and met friends at the mall.
Came across my purple ballet costume,
With leather toe shoes, I felt tall!
I found my jeweled tiara crown, put on some make-up
And mom's high-heeled shoes,
Reminding myself I can always dress up
Becoming a Princess whenever I choose!
MMM! From puddle-jumping in rain showers
Or warm sandcastles made at the beach,
To glistening snow angels, from fresh-fallen snow-
Nature's still within my reach.
How I cherish the wonder of Niagara Falls
Where real rainbows appear between trees,
In awe as the sun and mist dazzle my skin
Knowing the best things around are still free.
When the game of "Life" was fun to play
Or Chinese jump rope without mistakes-
To Easy-Bake Oven mini-miracles
Like cookies, pies and cakes!
Although she'd been away too long
It was very plain to see,

That sweet Susie still lives on in my heart
Mirroring the "inner child" of me.
Reflecting on rediscovering her that day
At a time when she looked the dullest-
I was given the gift of dusting both of us off
Pledging now to live life to the fullest!
Unleashing my long-lost passions
Keeps me centered when things can't get worse,
Forever weaving the tapestry of today who I am
With the courage to now put FAITH FIRST!
Next, I was filled with a sense of acceptance
By rekindling parts of my past I'd thought died . . .
As warm-fuzzies and love surrounded my heart,
And my "cup runneth over" with pride!
She sleeps on my bed to remind me each day
That life never happens by chance,
It's now up to me to make the conscious choice
For time to puddle-jump, shop, bake and dance.
As each new day dawns I am grateful
To our Heavenly Father and the angels above,
Since I've wondrously learned to work less and play more
With my children, my friends those I love.
Reminiscing with my precious Susie that day,
Taught me a Life Lesson unlike any other . . .
Being kind, first to me, gives me more energy

Embracing my destiny, as Mom, friend and lover.

So, as a woman today, when life seems too tough,

I search back through my memories and pleasures.

Though, I enjoy warm-fuzzy hugs and trips to the mall,

My "Angels on Earth" are MY TREASURES!

For sweetly knowing just how to nurture me,

With their gifts of hot tea, laughter and touch—

Forever being the secret behind my real smile,

I love you all so very much!

TIGER © 2001 KING FEATURES SYNDICATE

When Life Appears Too Big, My Friend, Scale Down and Get Small Again

Unexpectedly viewing our ventures through the inquisitive eyes of a child can be a wonderfully healing experience, especially at times when our seemingly encased emotions need to be expressed. Looking back during the comforts of childhood we were all once "pros" at fully living, loving and letting go. Yet, negatively now as "Amateur Adults," our necessary need to dawdle amongst our desires takes an all-around back seat to daily accomplishing it all. Though this is not a chronically worsening condition if we are willing to constructively change. Then, by daring to divulge our true colors while courageously altering our agendas, we become outwardly blessed with a life we are free to treasure, not forced to tolerate. Once we realize the rewards of readjusting our own roadblocks (as no one else can truly go on "spoiling our sunshine or ruining our rainbows" without our given permission), we allow our inner self's active imagination incredibly to flourish! While willfully combining the acts of precious playtime, along with running rampant in the heat of our heartfelt hobbies, we can't help but really prosper amidst a *Life Is How YOU Look At It* positive perspective. As an added bonus, once reinventing our reality based on the all-too-familiar sensation of free-flowing inner peace, serenity easily prevails after bidding farewell to our everyday juggles and struggles. And finally, by scheduling some time along the way for our "child within" to pray, play and celebrate each day; we sweetly unlock one of the best kept secrets for becoming balanced of all time, "When Life Appears Too Big, My Friend, Scale Down and Get Small Again!"

When Big Girls Get Butterflies— Reflections in the Magic Mirror

"Princess Ashleigh" (as I call her) and her big sister Adrienne moved in behind me about two years ago. Their mommy was getting remarried, her second trip to the altar. "Tricia" was tying the knot with my forever-single neighbor "Steve", who spent round-the-clock hours renovating his house to make his new family feel right at home. For months, neither of us got any solid sleep prior to them all moving in together. Though, deep inside I knew these late-night remodeling efforts were done as a gesture of love for his soon-to-be wife and three special stepchildren. Plus, the positive thought of Steve's long-awaited lover and instant paternity made it so much easier to go to work every morning, essentially sleep deprived. Above all, I was magically made aware that the best things in life have a way of appearing before our eyes at those times that we are loneliest and not really looking!

When Ashleigh moved in, she was just six years old. Like me as a child, she regularly dressed in purple and sometimes resembled a rag-a-muffin too! I have loved watching her happiness unfold as she fully enjoys the simpler things in life, like drawing with chalk, blowing soap bubbles or jumping rope with her silly sister. On other days I've witnessed this "whimsical wonder" riding her bike up over the speed bumps, racing around on roller blades or blissfully bonding with her new puppy. The magic of these moments still warms my heart with all-out memories of childhood closeness with my own little sister, while remembering also how we would softly hold hands and skip happily off down the street.

Even today, this enthusiastic angel likes to "race" me home through our connecting yards the minute she spots my Jeep round the corner. Somehow, Ashleigh always wins, and I'm guaranteed to find her winded silhouette sitting on my front steps in anticipation of my arrival. Then, this special second grader loves to rock with me on my lawn swing as we tenderly talk "girl stuff" while enlightening me sometimes that I am her "best friend." And, although my own daughters are bigger now, she and Adrienne love to hang upside down on my now-squeaky swing set and laugh, while I continue to carry on my love of nurturing children by passing out Popsicles to them as they play!

Meanwhile, this precious twosome would also "share their sunshine" at Poppy's house as well. Many times, while driving past his mobile home, I'd spot their cherished dolls or chalk drawings scattered about his yard just like we grandkids did many moons ago. This scenario would always make me smile, as I knew these "sweet next door neighbors" not only decorated his patio, but warmed his passion-driven heart. And, in return for his constant gray hairs, he never missed out on a chance to spoil any child with a handful of Gingersnaps always right before meals, and guaranteed fresh from his glazed, gold ceramic cookie jar.

Yet, during some of our lawn swing discussions, Ashleigh would confide in me the lowdown on her biggest fears. At one time, Mommy and her new husband were fighting a lot and it scared her, giving her "butterflies" in her tummy. Repeatedly, she was told, that it would be necessary to move out if they didn't get along better soon. Besides, Ashleigh loved her new life, new friends and new home making this sticky situation hard for any little girl to swallow. These are the times I would hug her close, stroke her hair and rock her gently as we swung.

After Poppy passed on in late August 2000, Ashleigh came to see me with a pressing agenda (unlike her usual pop-over visit to let me know how much I really needed to pick up my dog's poop). So, while bound and determined to get her point across, she brazenly knocked on my door. Next, I showed her to my living room where she began to state her case. She whispered how she had been worried about me as she'd witnessed how I had been grieving. At this awkward minute, Ashleigh asked me point-blank if I would be moving. Here, I answered her that "although I had already wrapped up my mission of getting my grandfather homebound to heaven" I did not know if I could live here anymore. As in the end I explained, how I was kind of lonely now without Poppy's calming presence to continue causing trouble with. Understandably she nodded, while her big brown eyes filled up with tears and our souls sweetly connected. Now it was her turn to firmly reach out to me, as I struggled with my own vulnerability—complete with the adult form of "butterflies" churning inside my stomach. Meanwhile, alert little Ashleigh had figured this out all on her own! My, how this "peace keeping princess" fully mirrored my life! From the little girl who ultimately feared the loss of her best friend, whose home situations weren't always happy leaving her woefully walking on eggshells, and finally, by reflecting upon how sometimes we face life's obstacles amidst only a wing and a prayer! For me, this meant putting a smile on my face, even as my bottom lip quivered with uncertainty over how my own future would be unfolding.

At this eye-opening moment, I elected to share with Ashleigh a warm and true story about when Poppy expired in our hometown, even as our hearts were seemingly saturated with sadness. See, something very special happened on the night of his first showing, which she and her family later attended. Remarkably, at this filled-at-times funeral home, there was a beautiful yellow butterfly making its way around the dimly lit room. While openly awestruck, we watched in amazement as this uninvited guest hastily explored the vivid variety of fragrant flowers honoring our gifted grandfather. Then, just as quickly, it fluttered across the area in a free-flowing dance of delightful twists and turns! Almost instantly, our unrelenting sorrow turned into uncontrollable giggles, as "the child" within us found this far too amazing to ignore! While also remembering how our Poppy had always lived with some special trick up his sleeve, we were spiritually reminded to relish life to the fullest. More important though, I had reawakened the life lesson that Poppy would have wanted us to stick together in his absence, since he'd most likely played a part in this magical moment anyway!

Over the next few days, we packed our suitcases and headed off for scheduled services in the state of Pennsylvania. As visitors and vigils continued, we proudly escorted our Grandpa one step closer to his cherished homecoming beside his beloved wife. To our amazement, that same yellow butterfly miraculously showed up, now haphazardly clinging to the corner of the room and appearing much more subdued. Yet once again, this "unexpected guest" still managed to lift our spirits as not only was this journey our final goodbye as our fun-loving grandfather was laid to rest, it was also his eighty-first birthday! Therefore, this bittersweet scene made my yearly memories of slurping semi-soft ice cream and sampling Peanut Butter Cake all the more precious, while being our first holiday without him to "eternally ever educate" us.

Yet, throughout these trying years, I'd sustained enough "earthquakes with aftershocks" to know that the tougher times in my life will always teach me something incredible. Even so, it was hard to imagine that anything good would emerge from this heart-wrenching mess, as dealing with death everyday doesn't usually bother us until it affects someone we deeply adore. Meanwhile, I simply handed my strife over to God's more-than-capable insight. First and foremost, I prayed for Him to send me both the energy and expertise to grapple through my grief. Second, I asked that He be lenient on my Poppy, as sometimes his "rosy sense of humor" could be a source of real thorns (something I'm sure Our Savior had already witnessed!) Finally, a feeling of sheer optimism overtook my sensitivities upon knowing things would now unfold exactly as they were supposed to end up!

When Big Girls Get Butterflies—Part II

Weeks later, in early October, I was driving home as usual. Like any other evening, Ashleigh spotted me and raced off towards my turf. Yet tonight, as I drove past Poppy's darkened residence, reality really reeked! At this very moment, I realized that my now-gone grandfather could no longer "erase" the daily pressures of my E.R. happenings (including hours filled with "Code Blue's" and some very determined plights of survival versus death) almost instantly with his home-cooked meals and homegrown happiness. Here, his firm hugs and freshly picked red roses would immediately shift my focus to the sources of love surrounding my own life, therefore releasing pent-up emotions without words ever being spoken. In the meantime, my precious little Ashleigh was patiently perched upon the patio when I pulled up in front of the house. "Uggh! Not tonight!" I thought, as I could feel a sudden migraine pressuring my eyes, causing me to even see spots. Then, while spiritually sensing that my overworked body was in need of some serious time of tranquility, I brushed past my "little princess" to plant myself upon the lawn swing. I placed my throbbing head atop my favorite pillow, and began to rock steadily in hopes that the waves of nausea would next somehow subside. At this point, I snapped at Ashleigh how she and Adrienne would need to go home, as my head felt like it was going to "blast off" from my shoulders.(Besides, they were giggling as always!) Since intuitively I knew that I not only needed to rest, but was both heartsick and homesick for Poppy amidst feelings that no one else could EVER understand how easily he could make any miserable day disappear. Before long, I had quietly begun to meditate, while delightfully remembering how delicious his ginger snap cookies tasted when dunked into cold milk. And, from within my trembling heart, I could still sense the warmth of his tender touch as he would pat my hand lovingly prior to handing me the gift of his precious red rose petals. Then almost magically, my headache began to ease up once discovering a way to still connect with Poppy's presence by sweetly "wallowing in our visits" amongst my vibrant visions. Suddenly, I felt a surge of relief run over my outstretched body as I gave myself permission to feel the pain of losing my loved one. On this exceptional day, I discovered tremendous spiritual healing simply by allowing my aching heart a sacred time out for my own illuminating "soul work" instead of always showing steadfast support for others enduring the same strides of life. And, in light of this *Life Is How YOU Look At It* wonder-filled reaction, what a difference choosing to be resilient made over woefully running for cover.

While checking my watch, only fifteen minutes had passed since I'd sent those silly sisters "scurrying southbound." And, just when I was about to drift into a peaceful dream-like sleep, I was startled by the pitter-patter of approaching little feet. As I struggled to open one sun-drenched eye, Princess Ashleigh approached from an angle and slipped something small into my scrunched up hand. "Here Nancy," she whispered softly, "This is for you." Then, after flashing her sweet smile, she turned sideways and skipped off. Once peering down into my palm, I next discovered that my persistent little neighbor had again tugged on my heartstrings by leaving behind one of those tiny custom cards, traditionally tucked within flower arrangements. The sentiment found at the top of the paper read "Happy Sweetest Day" while written in her second grade penmanship, she had secretly scribbled: "I Love You Nancy, Love, Ashleigh" on the front of this too-touching treasure. Even more magical, was the fragrant fact that three beautiful red roses were pictured right next to her meaningful message! I will never forget the wonders of this "warm-fuzzy moment" where my little rag doll knew exactly what I needed to end a less-than-perfect day, some comforting red roses wrapped in from the heart love!

Happily here, as summer 2001 unveils its elegant arbor, Poppy's patio rosebushes continue to bloom even without his hospitable presence. Likewise, while "bonding with nature" one aromatic afternoon, I was weeding beside my lilac bush as Ashleigh whistled nearby. Suddenly, we both watched in sheer awe as a beautiful, yellow butterfly rapidly approached us. Now, amidst moving softly from blossom to blossom—it had seemingly appeared out of thin air! Finally, it came to rest on the "empty ring finger" of my open left hand and slowly outstretched its wings. Next, Ashleigh gasped as we studied it closely, and noticed how its delicate three-inch wings were almost torn right in half! Softly now, she whispered that she was afraid that our "wounded butterfly" would never be able to fly again, due to its damaged wings. That's when I enlightened her to another tried-and-true tidbit Poppy had previously taught me. Positively, he would always encourage how: "Anything is possible Missy, when you dare to unleash your dreams!" With that, I lifted our injured butterfly slightly up over my purple lilac bush (while intentionally using these perfumed blossoms as a padded cushion in case it needed to "crash-land" at take-off). Meanwhile, I supported this unsteady insect until it felt safe enough to move off my stilled fingers and manage to fly again. Next, we both watched in amazement as our brazen Monarch-like butterfly became just a speck in the sun-filled sky! Yet, the memory of this sacred moment has touched my soul deeply, as it paralleled perfectly, how Poppy was always the wind beneath my wings. Then, Ashleigh's eyes lit up as she wondered aloud if he may have "sent" this special butterfly too—since we'd both experienced first-hand how the "sensation of fluttering butterflies" can be a fortunate thing! Here, I responded how I was sure that he did, with yet another awesome Life Lesson to be exposed before my eyes. Where wondrously, "the faithful examples of success-driven others can fill us with the courage to conquer the extraordinary, even at times when our own weathered wings seem too fragile to keep flying solo!"

That fateful day, as I continued my green-thumb efforts into my front yard's garden, another mini-miracle awaited. One of the really shriveled up he-was-too-sick-to-take-care-of rosebushes was now in full festive bloom! Even more remarkable, this once-transplanted remnant was alive-and-well for the wear, and had graced my awareness with three beautiful red roses! And, like millions of childhood times before, I knelt down beside these kindred keepsakes to savor their softness and scent. Next, tears of gratefulness to God and my grandfather streaked down my wind—blown cheeks, while gently falling onto each burgundy blossom, causing their petals to genuinely glisten while framed in the sunlight's finesse. Then, at this touching moment, I fully grasped the meaning behind Poppy's favorite "Serenity Prayer"—as acceptance, wisdom and courage are three awesome and irreplaceable values I wouldn't want to be caught without.

That afternoon when I willfully combined with nature, I also rediscovered the bliss of being totally content with my choices. More important, I knew that we "worldly girls" would not be moving out anytime soon—as this sturdy, white mobile home was still very much where we belonged. Moreover, God's Illuminating Guidance had shown me that my actual turf is anywhere that I can play "I Spy" by simply merging as one with manifested moments! Likewise, my energetic little Ashleigh shared how she would not be moving out either, as the Lord's faithful wisdom had firmed up the foundation of Mom and Steve's now-fading wedding woes as well. This unexpected outcome, truly based on new beginnings, gave my very special godsend back her girlish freedom to be the giddy, almost eight-year-old I definitely adored! Once again, I knew exactly how she felt. After all, we'd both managed to kiss goodbye our "butterflies of uncertainty." As an added bonus, I'd become the rejuvenated recipient of heaven-sent happiness since God's gracious revelation had answered my prayers with a comforting-since-my-childhood-mix of His serenity and sunshine to go! Yet, in the end I will always cherish the *Life Is How YOU Look At It* message of Poppy's gift within my grief, as I forever pledge to find a way to slow-up my world and stoop down more often to smell my "Reincarnated Red Roses."

"The fragrance always remains in the hand that gives the rose."

~ Hada Bejar

Peanut Butter Cake

(Caution: Allergy alert, this recipe contains peanuts)

Bake one 13x9 yellow cake mix and cool.
For frosting you will need:
A one-pound box of confectioner's sugar
About 1/3 cup milk (though may need a little more)
One "healthy" tablespoon shortening and
2-1/2 heaping tablespoons of creamy peanut butter
**Empty 2/3 box of confectioner's sugar into medium
mixing bowl. Next, fold in shortening and Peanut Butter.
Stir in milk slowly, to achieve desired consistency, and
carefully spread atop of cooled cake.
Grab a fork and enjoy!

(With special thanks to my late Aunt Nonie, who forever-brought a Peanut Butter Cake to every family function and always took this yummy recipe right off the top of her head!)

A Lesson in
High School Humility

A few weeks before the start of my Senior Year, my pre-arranged schedule arrived in my family's mailbox. While I scanned down the list of computer-selected teachers, I felt myself cringe with a burst of unhappiness. As luck would have it, I would once again be plagued with "Miss Pontecorvo's" English class as the final period to end my early dismissal day. Furthermore, this exact scenario had haunted me since entering LaSalle Senior High School almost four years ago. Likewise, she had always appeared last on my list, both as a wisdom-filled teacher and with my own attitude. Meanwhile, my mind reflected back to reading such boring books like *To Kill a Mockingbird* and *Macbeth*. These murky stories always left me wondering what useful purpose making me read them would ever serve in the footprints of my future, as I'd planned to enter a career in the health field anyway. Next, I recalled how I had only learned two off-the-wall things while in Miss Pontecorvo's ninth and tenth grade classes combined. Foremost, I knew the use of correct grammar inside and out, especially pronouns. Second, I'd more than mastered the art of sketching her on paper during school time on a daily basis. Here, her "impeccably-dressed-with-matching-shoes-pin-curled-stout-figure" always took on a "Miss Piggy" appearance, once my artwork was finalized. This would always make me giggle, as her real-life resemblance became almost comical when combined with her natural tendency to stutter and slur if she found herself flustered in class. Yet, Miss Pontecorvo passionately plugged along, while steadfastly believing that by some form of osmosis that she just might make a difference in our know-it-all lives.

During my junior year, we read more of *Romeo and Juliet* and *The Canterbury Tales* as mandatory assignments. At this point, Miss Pontecorvo would spruce up our studies with magical stories of medieval fanfare and Renaissance fashions, while now speaking a language even I could relate to! Besides, on my own time I loved to read anything with a romantic theme, while fashion finesse had become my forte´. Then, this thoughtful teacher began to push past out procrastination with individual expression like private journal writing. We also created group essay assignments, where she always critiqued from her chair in the corner and graded without a "curve." While she continually demanded quality work, I constantly dreaded being pushed to the limit. Somehow too, the social butterfly I had become liked laughter, love and long-term friendship more than sitting in study hall soaking up Shakespeare's sonnets! Meanwhile, I decided to coast through the rest of our readings, and simply slacked off on the quality of work both "Miss P." and I knew that I was capable of. And, although this swift change in study habits didn't reflect in my final report card, I'm sure she and I both knew the real score.

When my senior year began, I couldn't help but feel like Miss Pontecorvo's latest "prison sentence" had nothing left to provide me. (Here also, I had dropped out of a late afternoon typing class to once again trade "letting loose" for learning. And, as I sit here slowly typing today, it is still a much-regretted move!) Moreover, my most enriching life lesson would have nothing to do with her expertise of English, where sweetly too (like Aunt Nan and my Poppy) I'd been born with a contagious sense of humor. Therefore, I loved to make another's day a little brighter with something silly to smile about, even at times at the expense of someone else . . .

A Lesson in High School Humility—Part II

It was Halloween Day 1980, and I was bored in study hall. Though, on these approaching hours of spooky antics, I'd even brought some packaged candy to pass out to my pals. Before long I found myself digging through my purse where I willfully discovered a wonderful white Kleenex, and wrapped a round piece of gum inside. Next, I secured it with a strong rubber band that had just landed on my desk, after being "snapped" around the room by other students. Finally, I drew a large happy face on my homemade ghost then headed out into the hallway as the late bell began to ring. Upon entering the Empire of English, I spotted Miss Pontecorvo at the rear of the room with her back to all of us. Here, my friends and I laughed, as I leisurely flung that little white ghost onto her desk before taking our seats. Moreover, we had achieved a "new low" to making her class accelerate faster, even if she wasn't a willing participant! Yet, through all of this, I found myself torn between "fitting in with my friends" and facing the fact that there was really something I admired about her, both as a patient human being and a persistent bookworm.

One week later, a small white envelope arrived in my mailbox at home. On quick inspection, I discovered the return address to be from Miss Pontecorvo herself. Next, I found myself pondering just which words I would be using to explain my way out of this practical joke to my parents. After all, my Dad was a junior-high teacher with very little tolerance for any of his four children fooling around in class. Besides, I was sure Miss Pontecorvo was beyond peeved at me for pulling off this last-ditch stunt (that seemingly some "little snitch" had managed to let her in on). Meanwhile, as I tore open the envelope and began to read its contents, I was truly relieved! Neatly written in her tell tale handwriting was a beautifully composed "Thank you note." Yes, the kind I had learned to pen millions of times over in the prose she'd so perfectly taught. Now, her letter openly gushed about "the heartfelt gratefulness" she had experienced that Halloween Day amidst tidying up her desk to go home, when stumbling across my ghoulish ghost still waiting to celebrate this holiday with her. She further explained how her spooky start-up was so grueling from the get-go. Woefully, my saint-of-a-teacher had awakened with a sore throat, body aches and fever, and somehow decided to survive the school day even as sick as she was. To my further mortification, she wrote all about how she had witnessed me "whip something white" onto her desk from the back of the classroom, while never once realizing how we were all laughing AT her, not along with her. Finally, she praised me for being "a thoughtful and proper young lady." Then, to my crafty credit, that small piece of gum from inside her ghostly gift both managed to soften her holiday-deprived heart, and soothe her sore throat as she sampled this too-tempting treat. Thankfully here, I'd ended up doing something I could actually write home about!

Upon advancing to college, I was once again able to count on Miss Pontecorvo's pointers to make a positive difference in my G.P.A. See, as we reviewed the wonders of *Romeo and Juliet*, I remarkably learned how I had retained Shakespeare's work as if I had just scanned it yesterday! Never would I have guessed that her once-worthless techniques would remain useful in my college courses as well.

Looking back now, Miss Pontecorvo has played a vital role in shaping my success—both as a woman and a writer. Recently too, as my twentieth high school reunion approaches, I've thought of her much more often. One morning, as I was scanning our phone book for "Pet Poodle Groomers" my finger optimally landed upon her printed name. While believing as I do that "all things happen for a reason" I decided to give her a call. Once dialing her house, I was so pleased to hear that the colorful spirit of my favorite teacher still existed, even if only on her answering machine's recording, when I left my name and number. Blissfully, after "Miss P." phoned back, we made plans to meet at her house later in the week, where I would like to let her know what a difference she's made in my insights. Foremost, she taught me to always act the part of a lady, as I can never be sure who's watching! In addition, my own shoes always coordinate well with my matching outfits, as I last-minute dash out the door. Throughout the years as well, I have learned to lean solidly on my love of writing poetry and the reading of romance novels to make it through the tough times. And, today it is I, who willfully concentrates on completing these written works fueled by my own wonderfully colorful, *Life Is How YOU Look At It* relationships! Finally, Miss Pontecorvo's belief in me still shines brightly, allowing my heightened creativity to flow so freely. Yet, in the end, as my ink blissfully gushes with both her gifts of "good grammar and gratefulness" it is my turn to openly thank her. Though it has taken almost twenty years for this thoughtful and proper young lady to finally clear her conscience, I can't help but think that it's Miss Pontecorvo who forever got the last laugh!

Dare to Make a Difference by "Leaning In With Love"

"Carry a vision of heaven in your hearts
And you shall make your home, your school
Your world, correspond to that vision."
~ Helen Keller

I can remember as though it were yesterday researching and writing my fifth grade "term project" on the life and legacy of Helen Keller. Whether reading books, reviewing her quote collection, or silently watching *The Miracle Worker* movie; I was less swayed by Helen's "supposed handicap" and more mesmerized by the magic of her mindset! Incredibly too, although appearing outwardly disabled, she became overly determined to show each of us that we are all born special—totally gifted by God with our own "inner sparkle" that when allowed to truly shine, spills over onto anyone we take the time to touch. Here, I realized also, that we all have the option to view every encounter as "hopeful" instead of hopeless, while remaining only as limited as we allow ourselves to be! Yet, foremost I observed at the impressionable age of ten, how simple it is for any of us to become shamelessly disabled—when it comes to connecting, comforting or communicating with those seemingly judged less fortunate. As I watched Helen continue to thrive, I also learned to trust in my own heartstrings, treat better those deemed different, study sign language, touch Braille letters and tread with thankfulness in my travels. Since surprisingly also, those that seem the least like us sometimes have the most to teach! More enlightening to me though, throughout this entire divine experience was the expressed desire and emotional dedication of Helen's hard-working teacher, Ann Sullivan Macy. Where, as "a lady on a mission" she diligently portrayed a shining example of a true "Miracle Worker" by daring to make a difference in Helen's once so lonely life. Almost overnight too, this strong-willed teacher also taught me that although someone appears unreachable, they certainly aren't unlovable! And lastly, by finding a way to forever dissolve our barriers, everyone benefits; when we dare to risk rejection by reaching out to others and (as I call it) "Leaning In With Love."

With this thought in mind, fast-forward please to my first year of Nursing School at the age of nineteen, as already attending college though unsure of my health-related goal. Moreover, since Grammie and my Mom were both working as nurses (and I'd eternally been educated about "washing my hands and ever-wearing clean underwear in case I ended up in the Emergency Room"), I felt it only hereditary that I should follow in their footsteps. While growing up too, I would be forever etched the message that you were only "a someone" if you graduated from college. So, I decided to give Nursing school a try . . .

Dare to Make A Difference—Part II

It was a warm September morning as I pulled into the nursing home parking lot with the heat of the sunrise softly surrounding my shoulders (while considering this also to be a heaven-sent hug from my Grammie, as I knew she'd be proud of her "Sunshine" as well today). Meanwhile, as Aunt Nan had tenderly taught me too, I appeared properly "primped" – meaning primed, plucked and presentable. While simply dressed per protocol in my crisp, blue uniform, required ponytail securing my long, brown hair at the nape of the neck and polished white shoes so shiny they sparkled; at least from the wardrobe standpoint, I resembled the perfect example of a new nurse-to-be. Besides, while having recently passed my "bed bath exam" in class on a mannequin with flying colors, I felt beyond ready to put my skills to the test with a hands-on human.

After getting a brief history on my first-ever patient, I headed down the hallway with my "Care Plan" in hand. Upon entering the dark and chilly room, I spotted a tiny lady dressed in blah attire in a wheelchair next to her bed, and seemingly oblivious to my presence. At this point, I adjusted her blinds and allowed the warmth of the sun to shine in, while also shedding a "whole new light" on the subject. Why, of course my passive patient was unable to acknowledge me, as her eyes were so crusted shut she could not even see! As her half-finished breakfast tray lingered on the bedside table, I needn't question the fact that she had eaten (a requirement of my Care Plan) as this morning's soggy oatmeal was still smeared all over her face. She was truly a sight for sore eyes in her soiled hospital gown and messy white hair, while obviously "hurridly fed and hopelessly left to ferment." As her head hung stiffly at her chest in hues of shame and sadness, I began to prepare her bath. Yet, while walking past her closet, I spotted several silk pajama sets seemingly in mint condition with matching satin slippers. Once back beside her wheelchair, I placed the warm basin upon her nightstand and switched on a small radio on the now sun-drenched windowsill. Next, as "Wilma" was being serenaded by some classical music, I busily washed her up. First, I cleaned her once-stuck eyelids then freed up her food-spattered face. Half wishfully too, I wondered to myself "Who was this sad woman and was she at one time special to someone? Did her loved ones still care or was she forgotten by her family? And finally, if she could talk, what kind of story would she tell?" Now, I couldn't help but notice her sparkling blue eyes peering back at me as I crouched down to her level and continued on with her care. In the meantime, I smiled in the hopes of unlocking some sort of reply, as happily now, some nice harp-filled music helped to soothe the silence. As my little lady remained unfazed and her chin sunk further into her chest, my heart sank too—figuring my feverish efforts had failed me while falling on deaf ears. Then, after reaching into her nightstand in search of an extra towel I made a huge discovery! Even at her age, Wilma loved lipsticks, lotions and "looking female" almost as much as I did. Suddenly, I knew exactly how to reach her. After all, Aunt Nan had forever ingrained in me the nurturing principle of "never being too old to properly primp!" At the same time, the beauty of this moment made even more sense when the illuminating rewards of that perfectly-graded Helen Keller project allowed me to recall; "Just because someone appears unreachable, doesn't mean they are unlovable." In a heartbeat here, I revisited my patient's closet and picked out a pair of pretty pink pajamas. Next, I delightfully discovered "that in the time it would have taken me to throw on her required garb," she instead resembled a refreshed goddess! While proceeding along with Wilma's three-minute makeover, I then cupped her wrinkled chin in my right hand. Here, I added color to her lips and cheeks, lotion to her skin, and lots of hairspray to her unruly hair—making for the final touches on her now-pretty presence. Once finished, I emptied her bath basin and washed my hands in warm water (wouldn't Mom be proud?) and began contemplating the tasks of changing her bed and completing my Care Plan. But, as I returned to my passive patient, I could not help but feel like something was still missing. Though I had just brushed Wilma's "fly-away hair," it quickly appeared unkempt, hanging down over those now-vibrant eyes and blocking her fresh-morning view. Yet, this time while in search of a barrette or bow, I slipped my hand further into her top nightstand drawer and was shocked to discover another "comfort-quilt connection" from the pages of my own past! You see, emerging from a plastic package buried in the back was the same made-of-yarn pink hair ribbon that had been so tenderly tied around my own pre-teen ponytails! Meanwhile, as I again sprayed the silver hair of my tiny lady and tucked her wisps into stylish bow, just the feel of that familiar, Goody hair ribbon unleashed a floodgate of old memories for me.

Dare to Make A Difference—Part III

As I continued on to change Wilma's bed sheets, my thoughts centered around the warm-fuzzy magic of childhood closeness with my best friend, Diane, while also dating back to a sizzling summer scene in 1972. And, although inseparable at times since about the age of four, I vividly recalled our almost nine-year-old stint of daily peanut butter and jelly "porch picnics" with grape Popsicles for desert as we talked our passions and plans. Here also, Poppy would stop by and bug us, while telling me teasingly to "Be sure to eat your bread crust Missy, 'cause it will make your hair go curly." From that day on, after bursting out in giggles, Diane would always rib me about my lack of love for bread crust! Needless to say, when my pregnant mom snapped our picture that afternoon, the sun sparkled brightly on two smiling best friends, one in a forever-straight ponytail and the other in short, curly hair (while "photogenically" proving also, that one of us had actually listened to Poppy!) Now, as I reminisced through our younger years like a "View-Master" of my visions, I realized how truly special Diane was to me still. After all, there was no one else I'd rather gone through girlhood with! Whether learning to ride bikes, loving to "talk boys," or laughing at our endless stream of inside jokes; we forever spoke a language only two spirited soul-sisters could uniquely understand.

Yet, somehow, that scorching summer seemed to fly right by. Next, the reality of fall's arrival would find me nervously switching schools, to a new "smart kid's class"—though happily unfolding too, more lasting friendships and the truly life-altering miracle of Helen Keller's flair. But, no matter where our travels took us, Diane and I would always find our way back to each other and that wondrous warmth we shared. From snuggling in our sleeping bags at our first ever away-from-home Brownie trip, to waking me up as teenagers to smoke Newport's and swap the basic "do's and don'ts of dating" outside my darkened bedroom window; I could rest assured my secrets were safe with her in issues big or small! Yet, as we grew up slowly, we grew apart steadily as she was now concentrating on a new career and I was consumed with college. Meanwhile, that resurfaced ribbon had sweetly reminded me that it would do our hearts good to reconnect. Remarkably, I remembered how Diane's twentieth birthday was only a few days away, so I decided to grab a gift and go visit once my clinical day was complete.

Then, suddenly amidst plumping my patient's pillowcases, I felt an odd sensation send a chill up my spine! Upon turning around, I was startled to discover that this once-timid grandma had now reached out to me, and gruffly grabbed onto the back of my uniform! Next, I fearfully observed her waving her hands in front of her face, amid struggling to try to tell me something between a series of grunts and groans. Frightfully here, my first inclination was to "run from the room" until I was saved by *The Miracle Worker's* insight. Where, almost instantly I recalled, how the persistent teacher Ann Sullivan Macy had shown me to willfully Lean In With Love, especially amongst those situations where I'd really rather retreat! So, at this point, I forged past my patient's frenzied fingers. Then, once within her grateful grasp, she eagerly stretched her arms around my neck and gave me a really huge hug. Moreover, this sudden scenario still proved well from fifth grade; "Although someone appears unreachable, doesn't mean they are unlovable" even if it's me! In the aftermath of this awesome moment, my perspective on people was creatively changed—knowing this sad, "neglected nobody" had become somebody special to me! After all, she'd dared to make a difference in my destiny as her delicate gesture had truly caught me by surprise.

Next, as I swiftly exited the nursing home that day I couldn't help but feel like I had succeeded, learning less from a heartless mannequin, and more from a heart-shriveled human. Incredibly too, although leaving my little lady behind with a kiss, her Life Lessons I've long taken with me. On that day also, I had learned two very important things, as planning to become a parent down the road. First I knew, my cherished children would never leave home with messy hair and dirty faces. Second, I'd gained a whole new appreciation for my all-time favorite bumper sticker, "Be Nice to Your Children, They'll Pick Your Nursing Home!" Finally, once arriving at the mall to pick out Diane's present, I had found another way to celebrate the perfect day—by keeping that intuitive promise to myself and stopping over to see her. Then, as we refreshed our roots amidst genuine "girl talk and giggles" I above all knew, that life didn't get any better than this.

Leaning in With Love—On Wisdom, Womanhood And The Workplace

Little did I know, about one year from now, I'd be getting a "crash course" in reality while still thinking I had all the answers. Meanwhile, I'd become a newly married, first-time mom at the age of nineteen, and had planned to take only a year off from my Nursing studies to get our daughter off on the right foot. Sadly here also, Diane was involved in a serious car crash and since unable to overcome all her injuries, headed to heaven just days after her twenty-first birthday. Regretfully too, amidst these new winds of change, I never did get to flex my busy schedule again and freely wander over to visit. Therefore, while truly shocked amidst having to get ready on the morning of her funeral, I "semi-primped slowly" to say goodbye to my girlfriend. At the same time, I can tearfully remember asking to God, "How will I possibly find the strength to pull through this?" (After seeming to endure one hefty-heartbreak after another, as my own twenty-first birthday now waited in the wings.) Yet, once I arrived at the closed-casket service, the answer came easy. You see, even throughout her final farewell, the warmth of Diane's so "sparkling spirit" continued to work the room. Fortunately, for me also, my favorite childhood friend had still found a way to ensure that I'd smile. Miraculously here, the piped-in music played in her honor was none other than the "Best of Bread" collection (as one woman I know has yet to bond with her bread crust, while making those "summer of '72 porch photographs" even more priceless!) Remarkably as well this "Magicube moment" also gave way to the fact that although Diane had begun the sacred journey of "crossing over" already; our longstanding ties of love and laughter were gratefully still within reach. Foremost too, I've found that sometimes "Leaning In With Love" means letting go far too early, but not before we were lucky enough to giggle as we grew. Then, from this eye-opening awareness, I've also promised that "although the 'sensitive fires of friendship' can truly fade or flicker, it has since become a top priority to schedule time to fan the flames."

Today, though I never did graduate from college fate finds me pursuing the path of a "Sparkle Specialist" (since there is always something to smile about!), amidst pledging to pass along the magical-to-me teachings of four spectacular women: Helen Keller, Ann Sullivan Macy, that petite patient and my precious pal. Meanwhile, I have also discovered three more *Life Is How YOU Look At It* ways to enrich my world. First, I've learned that it doesn't take a degree to be decent. Second, it's up to no one on this earth to be the ultimate judge of my journey. And lastly, "If you put nothing into something, you'll get nothing in return," while truly missing out on the miracles in each moment!

On Wisdom, Womanhood and The Workplace—Part II

Yet, never have these Life Lessons become a more valuable teaching tool then in my health-related workplace over the past few years. Incredibly, since not having veered too far off from my original career choice values, the combination of really opening my heart along with upbeat radio music, make it so much easier to submerge in my surroundings during times of calm or craziness. So, each day as I thankfully advise a "spirited staff" of emergency room secretaries (while always wearing clean underwear!), I energetically emphasize how "seeing, listening and feeling" have a contagious side effect. Likewise too, I regularly reap the rewards of "Leaning In with Love" by staying focused on the present and showing patience with my patients. Somehow too, by setting the stage for success by willfully daring to care, I have easily noticed how each person is less apt to remember which line they needed to sign on, and more touched by an empathetic attitude, mixed with service with a smile!

But positively today, in whatever profession we practice, we would certainly all benefit in the "Heightened Esteem Department" by carrying out our callings with a Compassionate Care Plan, one consistently aimed at coworkers and others that we come in contact with. Besides, since this concept has been seemingly left behind in the cobwebs of our college curriculum, we could easily enhance our own waning ways by enrolling in a refresher course. Though, appearing in any job situation we've all witnessed those with hardened hearts and sour spirits, as some who are so busy inflating their own egos have shamelessly forgotten how to feel. Yet, amazing to me too, is the sorry appearance of those I call "the wafflers" in the workplace. These are our chameleon-like cohorts who appear sweet as syrup while working face-to-face with us, only to "soggily bend, break and back stab" the minute we leave the room. Then, to avoid appearing awkward in the eyes of others (by at times taking a brave, and sometimes solo stand), they instead wimp out by "waffling"—choosing instead to follow the tempo of the crowd over the true call of their conscience. So, by changing their minds more than changing their underwear, they unexpectedly provide a steady supply of Maalox moments for those of us left hanging, as they knowingly slide off the hook. Though seriously folks, while observing firsthand daily how we all defecate the same, there is no Hierarchy in Heaven for those with superiority complexes who make life hell on earth. More important, once we realize that we "needn't take anyone's power issues to heart" we free up our positive energy, allowing us to highlight instead the real happiness amidst our entanglements.

At this juncture, I smile as I recall how one of our favorite physicians shines brightly in my eyes while claiming ownership of his attitude. Respectfully, he always pens the word "please" after his written orders from lunch trays to lab work, while also realizing that he cannot be a faithful team player without a team that he has faith! By largely showing his appreciation instead of lashing out abruptly, he more than gets his point across—amid daring to do the little things that make a big difference in our day. And, although it requires an actual effort to reach out with respect to those closest to our cubicles, the rewards become well worth it—as one working amidst real value, reaps both productivity and peace. In the meantime dear readers, when was the last time you were greeted at work with, "Thank you for coming in today?" Also, why is it that some co-workers who are the biggest fans of the Sunshine Club (those that give you birthday gifts, send get well cards and forever pull together during funerals, fires and floods) are the first in line to give you grief when no one else is around? Wouldn't it make more sense to simply forego all the phoniness, and focus mainly on true fairness in the here-and-now? Just imagine how much more sunshine would actually be spread!

Sweetly as well, by creating a custom Care Plan for myself, combining touchable goals in the moment mixed with treasured dreams down the road, my journey as well continues to sparkle. Moreover, while still guided today by my "View-Master" of visions, I've vibrantly become someone I enjoy being instead of someone others would have liked me to become. I have also experienced the inner ecstasy of being doubly-blessed, as in the light of God's love, if I believe it, I'll achieve it! (Gee, I can almost hear Diane's lovable laugh once again, as those Life Lessons from being little still guide me with answers today. Yet, shocked she would be also, as I somehow too now sport a short haircut, have squashed my cigarette habit and have solidly set my standards above dating those who require obedience school. Though, the real fact remains that my bread crust is for the birds!)

Therefore today, as fate allows, I continue to practice "Leaning In With Love" amongst my prospering personal life, still seemingly full of surprises. And, after finding out the hard way how easy it is to avoid the "coulda-shoulda-woulda syndrome" about those we care about the most, I now strive to put my heart on the line in the essence of every encounter. Miraculously too, each time I took the major risk of "reaching out to someone who has truly touched my spirit," those butterflies of uncertainty have been beyond enlightening! Likewise, after acquiring an autographed copy of my most-cherished book ever, having my favorite country song crooned directly to me from center stage and hearing the sweetness of "I Love You too" from those that stir the laughter in my soul; I forever know that Leaning In With Love will never let me down.

Blissfully, it has occurred to me that we all possess what it takes inside to be Miracle Workers, having been born with both the "gifts and the gusto" to make an imprint on this Earth. Besides, the sweetness of success should be less about who we once were, but DARE to blossom into being! Even more amazing, when we assume responsibility for rearranging the pieces of our own personal pie into various passion-filled portions, we substitute living sadly "as is" for seeing life through eyes a-la-mode! Yet, here also, as food for thought, I can't help but ponder the following through my

Life Is How YOU Look At It lenses. If Helen Keller could have "visions," why don't the rest of us? Finally, while becoming less focused on how the world views us and more flamboyant about how we view our world, if your life's agenda is truly NOT sparkling, what aren't you doing about it?

> "The best and most beautiful things in the world
> Cannot be seen or even touched.
> They must be felt with the heart."
>
> ~ Helen Keller

In Loving Memory of Diane Jelen
(September 1963-September 1984)

Everything I Own

You sheltered me from harm
Kept me warm, kept me warm
You gave my life to me
Set me free, set me free

The finest years I ever knew
Were all the years I had with you

And I would give anything I own
And give up my life, my heart, my home
I would give everything I own
Just to have you back again

You taught me how to love
What it's of, what it's of
You never said too much but still you showed the way
And I knew from watching you

Nobody else could ever know
The part of me that can't let go

And I would give anything I own
Would give up my life, my heart, my home

I would give everything I own
Just to have you back again

Is there someone you know?
You're loving them so
But taking them all for granted

You may lose them one day
Someone takes them away
And they don't hear the words you long to say

And I would give anything I own
Will give up my life, my heart, my home
I would give everything I own
Just to have you back again
Just to touch you once again

*   *   *

EVERYTHING I OWN
© 1972 Sony/ATV Music Publishing LLC.
All rights administered by Sony/ATV Music
Publishing LLC, 8 Music Square West, Nashville,
TN 37203
All rights reserved. Used by permission.

When Life Sends Us What We're Lacking

It was fall 1995, and I began to take up "mall walking" as a way to alleviate stress. On one such afternoon, while some rain danced on its roof, I almost tripped over a sign placed strategically in front of a store. But, little did I know, as soothing music blared and ceramic angels beckoned, this day would change my life. Foremost, that larger-than-life sign would reveal how there was a "psychic lady" sitting inside who would be more than happy to both read my cards and review my chosen path. Strangely too, since having taken this walking route many times before, never was my urge so strong to see what else they offered as well. Within minutes, I would find myself seated right at "Lucy's" table, where she eagerly shuffled Tarot cards and talked of things that made me, me! Then, she also conveyed like clockwork that my marriage was crumbling, our second house was not selling and my cherished dreams were caught somewhere between the devil and the deep blue sea!

Weeks later, while mall walking, I would again run into Lucy, only this time out enjoying an evening with her mate. Then, while slowing my stride down enough to introduce me to her spouse, I was truly unprepared for all the "warm-fuzzy feelings" that I'd uniquely experience next! Somehow too, upon stopping firmly to enjoy the magic of this moment; simply standing face to face with her, felt like I was staring in a mirror. See, at this exact time, we were divinely dressed in long, red coats with leopard scarves tied around our necks, while also unleashing a feeling of déjà vu that would always permeate our encounters! Meanwhile, over the next few months, my meet-ups with Lucy continued to provide major hope for my healing heart—as she not only became my new mentor, but a special step-mom to me! Moreover, she also blessed my ho-hum world with two hugely "wicked stepsisters" whose contagious love and laughter helped me to continue to thrive! Then suddenly, amidst this surge of blind faith, my marriage strife somehow ceased (for now), that "other house" sold in seconds and Lucy's lean-on-me love kept me as confident as a little child learning to skate! Sweetly next, with our support also, Lucy would squash one of her biggest fears by becoming the sole owner of a busy spiritual store. Besides, between our womanly hot flashes and "hormonal stress-fests," the homemade brownies weren't bad either! And, for all the times we would laugh so hard that tears streamed down both our faces, Lucy would always hope that I would ultimately pen my usually hairy-canary adventures to help others to lighten their loads. Though, at the same time she would always tease about my love for my umbrella, since I never would be caught anywhere with one hair out of place. Therefore, we both knew that I had "stepped out of the box" the day I left it behind at her shop, only to rediscover how wonderful it feels to catch sweet raindrops with my tongue! (Yet, even now, that really floral Avon umbrella still lives in Lucy's decorated farm house, to forever remind my "mystical step-mom" of the day her chicken crossed the road!)

Miraculously, with all this abundant optimism, more fears would now be faced! Before I knew what was happening also, I was in search of a new place to live. At the same time, my two young cherubs had only one wish, as they wanted "to live by Poppy"—a feeling I wasn't so sure would have my best interests at heart. Then, with map in hand, I began to explore that old mobile home park, only to find after two days of looking, that I was a day late and a dollar short for the one I'd hoped for most. So, on that sad afternoon, I decided to slurp a red Dilly Bar and stop over at Poppy's for some hugs. Though unexpectedly here also, I somehow turned up the wrong side street. When wondrously before me, was a white-sided mobile home with an orange, neon "For Sale" sign, now right within my view. And, when I stopped for a minute to examine the lot size, I could almost envision my daughters' huge swing set happily at home here as well. Then, after a few more bites of my ice cream, I made my way up the steps to the door. Likewise, this angelic family was very kind to let me in without an appointment, as the owner had just had surgery and swiftly needed to sell the place. Next, as this fateful journey continued, I truly loved this little house! After all, the walls were painted in an array of lovely pastels, the kitchen was loaded with sunshine, and my girls' larger bedroom was tinted in lilac purple to boot! Yet, you can truly imagine my surprise as I made my way to the master bedroom, being even more shocked to discover how that awesome view from within my windows was actually Poppy's floral-filled backyard too! From here on, there was no turning back as the owner would let me in early to make this into a haven we'd surely all adore. Furthermore, as my creativity began to flourish, my frequent stress was replaced with a relaxed feeling of so serenely allowed to be me. At the same time, Lucy would opt to visit "my blissful spa" where I couldn't help but mindfully notice how I'd been blessed with such spiritual gifts! Incredibly too, once getting real with her point that "my floundering faith needed something so much firmer in which to believe in," amidst my budding family, foundation and freedom—I felt like I'd finally come home!

For the next few years, Lucy continued to share some of her humorous insights with my *Life Is How YOU Look At It* heart. So, if at any time I was feeling down, she'd always make me a hot cup of tea and remind me of how far I'd actually come (and if her details weren't all that convincing, there was always that dusty umbrella now stuffed in the corner alongside her couch!)

Luckily today, Lucy remains one of my biggest fans as she not only taught me worry-free tactics, but took some time out from compassionately tending her gardens, to truly caress my soul. Besides, no matter how busy I get, I can always hear her say, "Don't worry, the money will always be there, Nance" as her eternal Life Lesson of "Be careful what you wish for, Babe" echoes within my emerging written works.

How "Meister" Saved Christmas

The first Christmas with my girls in our new home was going to be lackluster, or so I thought! Money was tight, as I'd spent most of Fall 1996 turning on utilities, paying legal bills and entering "phase two payments" at the orthodontist; predominantly on a part-time paycheck. Throughout November, I tucked away a few special gifts for each of my daughters as the budget-friendly female I was slowly evolving into. Since my job situation was sort of uncertain, I made plans to use my final check in December to finish up my shopping mission. See, the holidays were different now as I would no longer be "harped upon" for buying other's presents or harmoniously need to hide my purchases to avoid an argument. And, while looking back over these people-pleasing years, my holiday memories had been primarily painful. At one time, I sustained two back-to-back Christmases without any packages from my partner to open. I was told I "didn't deserve any presents" right down to my empty purple stocking. Gratefully though, these negative experiences were a "true gift in disguise" as I was beginning to notice the not-so-gentle whispers of my own guilt-wounded heart, while merging with the momentum to become my own now-gifted woman! Next, I realized also, how I would rather live all by myself, than feel truly alone in the empty presence of someone who was supposed to life-long love me. Moreover, I managed to stash some loose coins aside for my most-impressionable sweethearts to surprise their single Mommy with some secret stocking stuffers, as my "six-year-old inner child" could not bear the thought of Santa skipping her again this year.

Upon remembering these less-than-perfect holiday happenings, I would always find myself longing for one of those breathtakingly beautiful Christmas trees on display each year, amidst the lights and laughter of my favorite mall store. Steadfastly though, I soothed my "child within" by seriously promising her that someday I would own one of these, straight from the pages of my personal wish list. How totally freeing it felt that SOMEDAY was finally TODAY, as this successful milestone marked the sacred beginning of new traditions in our mobile home! When together we purchased a seven-foot Pine tree and decorated it fully, with family finesse and Victorian flair. Here, the shimmering accent of pink and teal ornaments mixed wonderfully with our satin-like selection of jazzy garlands and just-tied bows. Delightfully too, the mystic gold angels and matching sheer snowflakes seemed to dazzle amongst a mirror-like image of dancing diamond motion lights, draped in the soft synchronicity of my year-round décor. To top it all off, a Celestine angel comfortably graced the top of the tree. Where her smile was as content as mine, as we both knew how lucky we were to be celebrating a serene and secure holiday season.

At this tender moment, the girls and I opted to explore my old ornaments as an eye-opening touch to our family-filled fun. As we inquisitively gazed into each little box, I immediately realized how these long-lost trinkets had each played a kindred role in the surely "questing towards enlightenment" kaleidoscope of me! We also found cute hand-made designs that included some tiny picture frames of my own pre-school pixies, during the days when I could still smooch their whole scrunched-up faces!

While I continued to unearth these timeless treasures, I especially adored my light-up collection of miniature doll and gingerbread houses all creatively garnished with sparkly crystals and candy canes. Lastly, I discovered Mr. and Mrs. Santa Claus snuggled warmly in front of their fireplace. And, as I curiously peeked right inside their picture window, I excitedly found that they still radiated with as much sweet emotion as the first time I'd laid eyes on them back in elementary school!

Over the years, my "collage of Christmas" continues to grow with cherished gifts from friends and family alike. Wondrously now, we are the proud owners of a purple hot fudge sundae ornament, the Pillsbury Dough Boy, and a tiny white poodle dressed in a seasonal scarf (a spitting image of our own dog, Pooh-Bear). Yet, looking "nasty as always" was my buddy, "The Grinch." Then, for a brief moment, I reflected back to those times when my own frost-bitten heart had felt as hardened as the one forever painted on his chest. On a happier note, my all-time favorite decoration is my moving Cinderella ornament, a recent birthday gift from my best friend Denise. She fits perfectly amongst those sacred reminders of objects sweetest to my soul, while also reinforcing that the next "dapper prince" in my life will be the one who deserves me. See, we are never too old for some fairy tale magic!

Now, as my daughters and I finished decorating the tree, I was struck by a mind-blowing thought! While each special ornament stood out on its own merit when merged with all the others, they truly sparkled as a group! Moreover, this Victorian tree reflected beautifully my own real-life victories, once regally trading hardships for happiness! Although my struggles were tear-filled at times, they successfully combined efforts of love wrapped in the warmth of friendship, surrounded by faithful angels and illuminated in sacred ribbons of God's eternal light. Next, I was led to the conclusion that this Christmas season would be more focused upon the presence of answered prayers, than the buying of anyone's presents.

Though in the end, it was Pooh-Bear (our temperamental toy poodle) who had the toughest time adjusting to our new Advent agenda. From his favorite spot on the couch, he watched intently while I placed a burgundy satin tree skirt around the stand itself, covered in plush teddy bears. Next, I arranged a small pile of presents atop of this festive addition, as my pre-conceived vision of the "perfect tree" had finally materialized with this pristine touch. Suddenly here, our frantic puppy jumped off the couch as the only family member left to contribute to the festivities. Then, in a split second, he leaped over the presents, slipped under the tree, lifted his leg . . . and proceeded to pee! Needless to say, that cute-and-cuddly tree skirt that had just saved my new teal carpet was soon history. And, while not willing to take any more chances, I uniquely stacked our unopened gifts onto the other half of my queen-sized bed until ultimately Christmas morning. Even funnier though, was Pooh-Bear's revealing Life Lesson to me. He made sure there wouldn't be a "prince" in this palace any time soon as there was "no room at the inn" amidst unveiling his clever gift that even clusters of Christmas presents can be used as a reliable birth control method! At this point, I was even more amazed to have spent big bucks on a pure bread poodle who couldn't tell the blessed difference between a real and artificial spruce. Yet, luckily after this little fiasco, Pooh-Bear got the drift somehow and left our family tree alone!

In the earlier part of December, we baked and frosted cookies, blissfully decorated our mantle and mirrors, and mailed out handwritten cards to all those "wonders" we cherished. Next, I experienced a major sense of relief that my first holiday alone in years was humming along hitch-free. Meanwhile, on Christmas Day itself, we maidens would be enjoying an early meal at mom's house. Later, I made much-desired plans to join Denise's spirit-filled family for diet-crashing desserts, as my daughters would spend time with relatives. Yet, deep within my cherished comeback attempt, I sensed that something was still missing, though I couldn't quite put my finger on it . . . .

How "Meister" Saved Christmas—Part II

The two weeks before Christmas were really hectic in E.R., and I had the bulk of my shopping to finish somewhere between all the hustle and bustle. Here also, while routinely checking my mailbox one night, I was in for quite a surprise! You see, my car insurance bill had unexpectedly arrived (after being seriously delayed by a crossed-out change of address sticker) and was dismally awaiting payment just a few days away. At this time, I knew we would have a tighter holiday than I'd hoped for. Yet gratefully now, my thoughts shifted back to the times I would instill in my girls the heartfelt gift of giving. Where, at the start of every snow-filled season, we'd faithfully remove two "less fortunate" children's name tags from that neatly decorated tree at our local supermarket. Then, my petite daughters and I would scour the toy stores for passed on presents, while positively teaching them the pleasures of hands-on helpfulness. Suddenly too, I felt a "total twinge of truthfulness" as my own mini-elves could no longer afford to help Santa to lighten his load this year. Lastly, I tried not to dwell on the fact that we somehow too seemed "less fortunate" this Christmas.

Naturally, I was not alone in my pre-holiday distress. One of my favorite doctors, "Perrymeister" was outwardly stressing as he hadn't begun his total week-before-Christmas whirlwind of shopping. And, if this little detail were not enough to lose sleep over, he would also be working a bunch of twelve-hour-days between attending some wake and burial services for a family member as well. Yet, even amidst these unexpected events, he continued to write down his gift selections from the pages of coffee-stained newspaper ads, as he plugged on overwhelmed throughout the day. That's when

I walked by and casually tossed out that if he "carefully made up his list and checked it twice," I'd be more than happy to complete his family's *Life Is How YOU Look At It* shopping on my upcoming weekend off.

Once assuming the role of last minute Gift Goddess, we met at Lucy's store late Thursday night where I picked up Meister's wondrous wish list, and was impressed with the sensitivity in which it was planned. After all, he knew just what styles, fragrances and gift certificates his wife and daughters would enjoy. He then provided me with minimal shopping guidelines for his loving mate, "Only one flannel nightgown, please, anything with frogs and no Granny panties 'cause she hates them." Lastly, he handed me both his lengthy requests and an envelope lined with cash, to make his holiday blitzin' mission become a reality. Then, surprisingly as I turned to leave, he slipped me another white envelope. With a wink and a smile, he softly explained "Here's a little something extra for your own Christmas, Spike." Stuffed inside was surely enough to pay my soon-to-be-due car insurance, while also "unwrapping the gift" of being able to finish my own children's shopping! Miraculously next, my girlfriend Sarah and I traveled to three malls in two days—spending Meister's money on tasteful treasures. Meanwhile, he stayed busy making sure we hadn't bolted to the Bahamas, while seriously questioning his decision to let two "Shop-till-we-drop" ladies loose to heed the call of the mall! Next, we wrapped his selections like crazy and placed them in gorgeous holiday bags. Then, as promised, I delivered them on Sunday after loading up my sleigh. Humorously too, one of our nurses even teased that "it looked like there was a drug deal being exposed outside on the ambulance ramp," as we'd managed to exchange his "Santa stuff" straight from my overflowing car into his over-sized trunk in only a matter of minutes! Moreover, I don't know if Meister was more shocked to be saved by his once-shy secretary in surely record time, or that he really had some change left. Six cents to be exact! Yet, I too was shocked by following my sixth sense. See, throughout my hospital work years, I have attended mandatory in-services. Today, I smile, after being taught the cherished concept that, "Sometimes leadership needs to change hats." As in a heartbeat I'd chosen to tune into his apparent needs with my intuitive heartstrings, instead of letting the fact that he was considered higher up on the hospital hierarchy affect my decision of being "allowed" to assist him. After all, he was a doctor being human, and I was his secretary born to help out.

That Christmas Eve, as I placed the gift of Meister's Christmas bonus envelope into my now-filled purple stocking, I was overcome with tears of joy. For the miracles of this holiday season weren't to be found nestled under my tree, but nurtured within my own heart. Incredibly, once daring to merge in the moment with a too-much-to-do doctor, I magically discovered the treasured foundation of a fabulous friendship that Meister and I still savor today. This experience has taught me well to give of myself unconditionally, not just at Christmas time, but all the time. Besides, when the universe responds back to me with gestures of warm-fuzzy kindness, it's like adding "tons more mini-marshmallows," to my life's already overflowing cup of truly miracle-blessed hot chocolate! Sweetly too, in the end I've been shown firsthand how even Santa may switch hats. While helping to resuscitate "Spike's sagging spirit," I wholeheartedly have witnessed that sometimes he wears scrubs and a stethoscope!

*** In Loving Memory of Pooh-Bear
January 20, 1994-July 25, 2009.
A pet too special to forget!

Taking Time Out for
Guaranteed Giggles . . .
And "Tidbits" I've Been Told

*** A simple lesson in lady-like etiquette from my Grammie.
Men fart and women "fluff"'—need I say more?

One morning in December 2001, I headed off to our local mall as a maiden on a mission. I was also reminded how quickly, at times, the universe responds back to our requests with exactly what we've asked for. On this particular day I was in search of a pretty teal-colored hat to match my long, wool coat. I was also hoping for one more "silly story to cross my path" as a unique touch to this section, a pre-Christmas gift I would unknowingly unwrap just by staying present in the upcoming mall moment!

Once inside the main shopping area, I could feel my favorite upscale store beckoning me one step closer to buying my color-coordinated chapeaux! When suddenly, about fifteen feet from this stylish store's entrance my concentration shifted to the here-and-now. Next, I observed what resembled a middle-aged mother and her teenage daughter walking towards me, both bearing "constipated looks" on their concrete-like faces. Intuitively, my ears perked up in the hopes of discovering the real reason behind their "masks of miserableness." Then, I heard the younger woman ask in a disgruntled tone, "Why is it that most sales clerks at perfume counters seem so stand-offish and so snooty?" Knowingly I smiled, as I too had experienced a similar fragrance faux pas! One time, when actively portraying "Meister's Gift Goddess" that first awakening Christmas, I found myself unusually dressed in faded jeans and a flowing sweater. Then, while attempting to buy his wife a popular fragrance set at a pricier place, I further recalled how no one behind the counter could even be bothered to acknowledge me. That was, until I pulled a "not-so-petite" perfume and pearls jewelry box down from the decked out display, then whipped out a wad of one-hundreds to pay for it! Incredibly here, I was even offered the luxury of having my package wrapped for free! Needless to say, after overhearing those two less-than-thrilled ladies along with reliving my own "fragrance counter flashback," I thought I'd been blessed quite early with my excitement for the day. Yet, this divine timing was just the tip of the totally drowning Titanic.

Upon continuing along with my hat hunt, I scurried past the busy "perfume misters"—as at times my sensitive asthma doesn't appreciate those "sometimes pushy babes" spritzing me with spray bottles! Once arriving at the accessories department, I instantly zeroed in on my newest winter wardrobe wonder. And, amidst trying on this gorgeous teal hat and gotta-have glove set, another customer commented on how especially lovely I looked. She further remarked how amazed she was that not one little hair on my mega-gelled head remained out of place, even when I'd removed it. I also found myself grateful, as I would never get caught with a serious case of "hat head" that genuinely squished my spikes! Now, content with my selection, I began to gravitate towards the cashier before stopping off to admire some sparkling costume jewelry. Then, while browsing through the rhinestones and ruby slippers, I also witnessed that same snooty sales clerk be "once again anal" to another prospective perfume purchaser. When I surveyed the situation further, a few more "early birds" had arrived and one older woman instantly caught my eye. This stunning lady was perfectly dressed in a plaid skirt and colorful hose, while all wrapped up for winter in a flattering fur-trimmed jacket that ultimately fell to rest on the tops of her trim thighs. Here, as well, I could only wish to look so elegant in my own eighties! Now, with the help of her cherished cane, she was slowly inching closer to the "perfume vixen's" counter. And, as I held my breath in anticipation of her becoming the next "shark snack," something truly amazing happened. From about four feet away from the fateful fangs of that dismal diva, the eccentric missus let out a "rumbling fart" that easily measured at least an eight on the earthquake Richter scale! Meanwhile, this elder's timing could not have been more perfect. As in a flash, the "perfume poophead" now dodged behind her display so frantically searching for some sort of scent to squash her stinky surprise! With this optimal view, I openly laughed hysterically, since witnessing firsthand how we always get back what we give out and then some! To my delight also, my own wish had been granted. After all, I knew this karmic life lesson would be the perfect addition to my other awesome *Life Is How YOU Look At It* surely made-to-order miracles! Besides, after once again hearing my step mom say to me, "Be careful what you wish for, Babe," I was boldly reminded that not all Christmas bonuses contain mounds of cash or calories—but in the end may be our just desserts.

A picture of me, Mommy
(AKA "Spike"). 1997

Taking Time Out Gratefully for Some "Motherly Moment" Giggles

If there's one thing I know about having two children, I'm not the first parent to have heard, "You like her better, her piece was bigger and why can't I stay up later too, Mom?" So, in fairness to both my females, I've included an equal piece of both their pasts to enjoy.

This was not our typical Saturday full of grocery shopping and getting things done. Instead, it would be the evening of five-year-old Bethany's Christmas caroling concert. While this whole afternoon would seem to "fly by," it would soon become time to get her dressed and get moving. Though, for "just a few more minutes" I allowed my out-of-breath daughter to wriggle around on the carpet as she played with her now wound-up puppy. When suddenly, little Pooh-Bear made a dash for the doorway! At the same time, our showstopper-to-be got clunked in the mouth by someone else's knee! As a result, one baby tooth was left "hanging by a string" and the other turned seriously semi-sideways. Therefore, you can only imagine all the laughter from the audience as our youngest daughter delightfully belted from the stage "All I Want for Christmas Is My Two Front Teeth" while flashing a true, toothless smile! Meanwhile, amidst her aqua laced pajama set and Happy Holidays grin, these cherished words would become her "theme song" for way more months to come. Wow, if only all our must-have Christmas lists were so easy to fulfill!

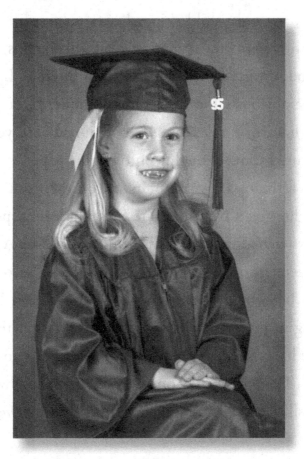

Bethany Nicole, Age 6

June 1995

My petite daughter, Michelle Marie, was a bright three-and-a-half year old with big, brown eyes and spiral ringlets within her thick brown hair. At this age, she was already reading simple books with ease, and welcomed the challenge of "sounding out" any unknown words. One afternoon, as she and I shopped, Michelle curiously amused herself in the children's book bin while her Mommy browsed nearby. Then suddenly, my only child skipped over to me with her eyes wide with excitement. In her porcelain-like hands, she held a small book with a tiny metal lock on the side. Incredibly, while she obviously found this item unique, I found myself filled with warm-fuzzies too. After all, it had been years since I had poured secret thoughts onto private paper in the same precious format, yet with a rainbow on the front! Next, as my daughter read from her rare find, she easily spelled out the letters etched in gold on its front cover, "D-I-A-R-Y," to the amazement of other onlookers. Moreover, seconds later, I would be convinced that my daughter would be surely following in my medically-based footsteps, as at the top of her little lungs she let everyone within earshot know, "Look Mommy, DIARRHEA!" Somehow too, this has always been the one silly story I should have sent to *Reader's Digest*.

Michelle Marie, age 4

Christmas 1987

My Saving Grace Grandpa

For four years before Poppy died, he found himself really busy! After all, he had us "fake it till we make it ladies" to teach the finer points in life. Remarkably, I became a class act at mowing the lawn "his way" and slowing down over the speed bumps to be able to savor his love. While his lectures would become less regular and I had budgeting down to a science, there was one issue I still could not get right. So much so, that it would really put the fire in his Fruit of the Looms each time I would run out of toilet paper. Then, he would always say, "Geez Missy, you need to plan for this stuff. Can't you just stop off after work for a twelve pack of Scott tissue instead of spending $2.99 per roll at the corner store up the street?" At this point, I would add further hype to my case by humorously asking each and every time, "But Pop, why should I stock up on extra rolls of the white stuff when I can always just borrow from yours?" Next, he would forever roll his eyes in the hopes that I might someday grasp the concept of planning for a rainy day. Here also, my girls were shown how "life is more about the family stuff," like old home movies, "Mickey Mouse pancakes" and playing card games from the heart. And each night, my daughters would join him for two handfuls of Gingersnap cookies fresh from his treasured cookie jar, as mom would de-stress upon the treadmill while being serenaded by Mark Wills' star-studded voice. Yet, at this time too, I couldn't help but wonder why my Poppy didn't practice what he preached. You see, he was the total "King of Frugal" before it was considered cool by saving all his brown paper bags, anything made of plastic and those annoying little twist ties in case there was a need. Meanwhile, he truly knew, that for every item that he could scrimp on meant more money he could surely deposit in the bank!

One day, as Poppy's "countdown to heaven" appeared to be inching closer, he invited me along to help complete his DNR. And, once leaving the doctor's office, he ordered himself a Denny's "Grand Slam Breakfast" while I thought I was going to barf. Here, amidst repeating his favorite childhood stories, I saw an obvious example of a man who wanted to die, while this struggling granddaughter was left hoping for thirty more years of his "Depression-era folk tales" and those divine, red roses off the trellis. But, happily as well, he'd become my cherished "father figure" by never bailing out on us when times had been so tough. Besides, no matter how hard I needed to work, my girls never had it so good. Even our tiny poodle, Pooh-Bear, was treated just like royalty—from car rides to McDonald's regularly for cheeseburgers, and once even snatching two huge pieces of Poppy's left all-alone pizza pie while he'd snuck off to take a leak. Therefore, while I was forever enlightened how "boys will be boys," we babes had our hands full.

As winter 1999 approached, the girls and I stumbled across the perfect Christmas gift for Poppy. After all, he was now known as a "dog hog" for no longer coming over to pluck Pooh-Bear each day from the stillness of our house—to finally just "stealing" his sweet little presence and keeping him all to himself. So, shocked Poppy was to be given an exact ceramic image of our precious puppy to now reside upon his fridge. And, while he never did return Pooh-Bear timely to "our palace," we girls had found an awesome way to one-up him for his jokes.

When the summer of 2000 arrived, my "caretaker cousin" would ring my doorbell at our ailing Grandpa's request. Here, "Rachel" was starting to obtain a list of belongings each loved one would want once Poppy would sadly depart. Yet, for me, this "wish-list" was short and sweet. In a heartbeat, I knew I would be honored to inherit his "Missy poem" and would incredibly love the rocking chair in which he'd always rocked me to sleep. Then, for my daughters, I would gratefully ask for his soft pillows and satin blankets for all those times they would play hooky, making "tents out of sheets" filled with grilled-cheese triangles and Tupperware toys instead of going to school. Finally, I'd also hope for a few of Grammie's treasured knick-knacks, his kindred cookie jar for our bottomless Bethany, and his mini-version of a radio to replace that AWFUL boom box Michelle always balanced on the edge of the tub. Likewise, as Poppy had hoped to "ensure equality," the rest of the family would be making their lists too. Though, once our grandfather's gentleness faded, some greedy egos still ravaged in like seagulls spotting supper!

Once Poppy's fight ended, I found myself removing precious photos off his fridge to take to the funeral home. From beneath his magnet collection as well, I took several pieces of artwork that would make any grandpa smile! When suddenly amidst "the chilling kitchen silence," that ceramic toy poodle caught my teary eyes. Where naturally, if Poppy couldn't take our Pooh-Bear along, he would want the next best thing! Therefore, you can only imagine the laugh we girls got, as the funeral home stuffed that silly poodle into the satin of his coffin before they closed the lid. Meanwhile, once arriving for more services in the nearby state of Pennsylvania, neither Poppy nor his "partner in crime" were any worse for the traveled wear. Besides, how much easier it was to see our patriarch headed off to heaven with that perfect little "comfort quilt" nestled by his side. Positively too, once these services were done, the ride home was so lighthearted, as we *Life Is How YOU Look At It* giggled over the silliness of our prank! Moreover, for all the million times our Poppy had encouraged us to "seek pleasure in the simple," we had more than made him proud.

My Saving Grace Grandpa—Part II

Though, in the next few months, I became increasingly aware that life is "less about growing old gracefully" and more about the Grand Scheme of things. You see, Poppy's plan to exit was not only based on when he, himself was ready; as Michelle now had her driver's license and my littlest was latchkey free! Sweetly too, while fall would next appear with its natural calming colors, even his trusty Craftsman lawnmower would find a home within my shed. Meanwhile, once these precious tapestry threads would seemingly come full circle, I was ready to put these stressful months behind me and manifest some inner peace. Here as well, I'd get back to my "spiritual basics" by breathing life into the dearest of things as Poppy had done with me. Therefore, you can imagine my surprise one night when Cousin Rachel from Canada rang my doorbell again. Next, she went on to say how in this doubled, brown paper bag she'd carried from over at Poppy's were several "deemed worthless to them items" that the "seagulls" never snatched. Then, after hugging her goodbye, I went back inside to enjoy more enlightenment from our always-prepared Poppy. First off, I removed one of those black-speckled composition books I had so regally learned to budget in. Upon snuggling it close to my chest, it still had Poppy's name inscribed precisely on the front. And, while he would also pen the year of "2000 . . . through whenever," this would be the very paper upon which my book would one day gush! Next, I discovered way more of his "surely anal personality" from inside my sudden package, as I was also the recipient of a flashlight with working batteries, a second set of silverware and that Teflon "Mickey Mouse Pancake griddle" that always made my hungry ones grin. Willfully as well, I sat down upon Poppy's soft brown rocking chair to bask in all I'd been blessed. At the same time, I found myself smiling as he still had found a wonderful way to make sure we'd be all right. Then, amidst rocking steadily, I reflected upon all "those uphill times" when Poppy's unique wisdom was just the thing to keep us girls going strong. Besides, from all those many tales he'd told, someone always had it worse! When suddenly, my daydreaming would abruptly come to a halt as the timer in the other room signaled how our dinner was soon to be done. Though, before I escaped to the kitchen, that "bag bearing gifts" again caught my eye. After all, Poppy had forever taught me to clean the house as I went along. So, while gathering up this "comfort quilt," I would be in for another surprise. As I started to fold this crumpled bag right in half, there was something soft still stuck inside. Blissfully, I was now the proud owner of that "familiar crocheted toilet paper doll," complete with a fresh roll to boot. And, while placing this aqua tapestry thread securely behind our pink toilet, I *Life Is How YOU Look At It* realized just how far I had actually come. Moreover, from stolen poodles to the "poop paper patrol," my Poppy may have left this world, but his antics still light up my life!

Families really bow their heads to pray
Daddies really never go away
Woah, oh, grandpa, tell me 'bout the good old days

~~~~~~

Poppy and Grammie—
taken around 1940

The Gifts of "My Grandmas"

It was fall 1976, and my turn to take care of my ailing "Grammie"—while also providing Poppy with a very much-needed break. Besides (in my teenage mind), since I'd been taught so well to baby sit, exactly how hard could this bonding time be? After all, it was "Eva" who'd shown me the most about lady-like style. Amidst her late night pajama parties, leisurely painting ceramics from the mold stage to a masterpiece and lovingly preparing yummy homemade cakes and cookies—she always smelled so sweetly of her signature Jean Naté lotion. And, if she were not having fun pursuing her hobbies like hunting, gardening or traveling with Poppy, she was working with her much-adored patients in a pair of perfectly polished white nurse's shoes. Yet, somewhere between all the hugs and the helpfulness, I was instilled with a sense that "anything I could envision was possible," as long as I threw some elbow grease in! But, more than anything that morning amongst my role-reversal from dearest granddaughter to designated guardian, I aimed to make her proud. By first, forever "fetching her pocketbook" and then fearlessly preparing her lunch as she'd been teaching me how to cook.

Yet, upon my arrival to Grammie's house, no amount of expertise could ever have prepared me for the unexpected Life Lesson I'd encounter next, which was all about paying the ultimate price for our personal choices. You see, the crippling illness of Emphysema would wreak havoc upon her beauty, once endlessly opting to chain-smoke cigarettes over being comfortably able to breathe. Here too, I sadly observed my once-busy Grandma become "couch-bound" while chained to her non-stop machines. And, as I tinkered next with her oxygen tanks (that were almost as tall as I was), I was less fazed by the word "Flammable" on the sides and more afraid of losing her love! Looking back through the years, she was always the one with the "Happiness Strategies" like handwritten letters from her heart made of gold—and would eternally call me "Sunshine," especially when my world needed a lift. Meanwhile, last year's so-puzzling actions of my precious Grammie had begun to make some sense. Since keenly aware that she was dying, I was the one, out of many much-loved grandkids to be blessed with her childhood china last Christmas. At that time as well, I also received a stunning ceramic doll she'd sculpted, that had some very precious-to-me words inscribed right on the bottom of her bright yellow petticoat. But, during this eye-opening moment, it also occurred to me "could it be she was somehow hoping to have my cooking skills conquered before humbly exiting from the ends of this Earth?" Then, once my intuition faded, I went over to snuggle my now-gasping Grammie, while pulling back her soft hair and applying some much-needed powder to her perspiring face. At this instant, I began to sing *You Are My Sunshine* to her just as we "never-too-old-to-learn ladies" had always loved to do. Though, in my trembling heart I prayed that even if she couldn't accompany me this morning, we girls would be o.k. Next, I helped my struggling elder to scuff her satin slippers off in the direction of her prized powder room, making this "once simple journey without an oxygen leash" a seemingly uphill task. On this day as well, the mood would be much different as Grammie's condition ultimately worsened and her responsiveness regressed. Next, as morning's sunlight streamed upon us, I proudly placed some warmed up Chili and a piece of her cinnamon-topped "Poor Man's Cake" on a tray for her to tackle. When suddenly here, she turned into someone I had never seen before! She crudely began to criticize me for making her lunch too hot, while also letting me know at the top of her charred lungs how I "would never make it as a cook in the kitchen or as a nurse-to-be in college!" Then, while these uncharacteristic words would painfully bruise my conscience, I placed a call out to my mother to aid in managing the backlash. Now, as the clock stood still, Mom finally arrived to soothe away my tears, while also reassuring me that Grammie's now-delirious state was nothing I could have controlled. Yet, if truth be told, the wounding to my self-esteem had already been established, but would take me many more years down the road to even begin to come to terms with. And, later that night as her situation shifted, Grammie was brought to the hospital amidst wavering in and out of consciousness. Though, at one time of extreme alertness, "Magnolia" (as Poppy would always lovingly call her) expressed a deep desire to have me brought before her as she so wanted to apologize for that ugly, earlier outburst. Meanwhile, my Mom had made the judgment call not to subject this middle-school daughter to any more upheaval, while surmising at this time also, that I was already asleep. Though at home as I lay wide-eyed amidst a river of racy afterthoughts, I was suddenly soothed by a "right-to-my-soul sensation" that Grammie's suffering had surely ended and that we could both now rest in peace! So, it was no surprise when Mom returned to say that we had lost her, as I'd already been enlightened that she would not live till the light of day. In the meantime, this would be my first experience in having a dear one die, yet wishing I'd done things differently. Moreover, I was so angry with my Mom for not giving me the chance to heal all the hurt I was left holding since Grammie never did get to from-the-heart apologize or have the chance to say goodbye. Though, in looking back now from a womanly perspective, the age of thirteen is a very tough one, between wishing you were bigger and wanting to stay small. In retrospect also, while slipping into Mom's shoes, I suppose my own much-shaken teenager would have stayed tucked within her covers instead of heading out into the darkness to resolve this death's door rift.

The Gifts of "My Grandmas" Part II

Luckily now, into my Lady-hood, I've learned to release a lot of my "supposed shortcomings," while living comfortably with the fact that although I never really wanted to be a like-the-rest-of-the-family nurse, I love surrounding myself in others who so spiritually need a lift! Somehow though, I've had a harder time perfecting my cooking skills in the kitchen as seemingly each time I'd attempt to prepare even something really simple, Grammies painful "chili conversation" would regretfully replay! Yet, happily here, I also discovered that hands-on healing doesn't happen without the help of someone else. Therefore, you can only imagine my surprise when a charming Senior Volunteer by the name of "Mrs. Sawyer" appeared one morning at my work desk—and softly tapped me on the shoulder to ask, "Excuse me dear, but where shall I put my pocketbook?" Furthermore, if that were not enough similarity to give me the goose bumps a definite déjà vu would always enrich my existence every Tuesday when she showed up. Especially since, she always brought in a small loaf of "cinnamon-sprinkled coffee cake" fresh from the oven for us to sample. Over the next few months I'd honestly grow to love her, as "this awesome lady in her eighties" would surely make my day! Though at first, it was hard to pinpoint exactly what I admired most about this so-obvious treasure. That was, until she began telling me wonder-filled stories about her children, her cooking and her career; while always wearing a pair of perfectly-polished white nursing shoes! Above all, for the many times she'd hug me close and I would kiss her so-soft cheeks, I couldn't help but notice her sweet resemblance to my own so-spirited Grandma. That's when I found the strength to confide in Mrs. Sawyer my nagging dilemma of never being fully taught to cook, since Grammie had sadly somehow died before we'd solidly finished. Then, from here on, every Tuesday she would come accompanied by a few hand-written recipe cards, like easy stuffed peppers and exquisite pound cake for me to experiment on at home. And before long, you guessed it—I'd mastered my fear of failure by preparing a variety of dinner and dessert ideas for my own family to enjoy. Moreover, while being adored like a real granddaughter in the arms of her welcoming world, I realized how I hadn't just needed a cooking course to succeed, but the comfort of someone watching over me just like Magnolia used to do! Meanwhile, I still happily carry a purple and yellow, *You Are My Sunshine* key chain that I stumbled across in memory of Grammie's homespun magic. Yet even today, while the sight of those large, green oxygen tanks still gives me the shivers, I've successfully learned as an angel-in-training, that it is "o.k. to have our stuck points" that over time will need some work. As for Mrs. Sawyer and I, we still remain close. Since down the road too, my cherished turn would soon come to be her "Saving Grace" also, through one of the scariest times of her life!

Grammie's Poor Man's Cake

- PREHEAT OVEN TO 325 DEGREES
- SPRAY OR GREASE AN 8 X 8 PAN

* IN A LARGE BOWL COMBINE:

2 CUPS FLOUR
1 CUP SUGAR
2 TEASPOONS BAKING POWDER
1 TEASPOON SALT
1 TBSP. SOFT MARGERINE
I CUP MILK

* MIX TOGETHER AND PLACE IN PAN
COVER BATTER WITH ½ STICK MELTED MARGERINE
LASTLY, USE 1/4 CUP SUGAR WITH CINNAMON TO TASTE
AND DRIZZLE OVER TOP

BAKE FOR 20 MINUTES AND ENJOY!

* FOR A FRUIT-FILLED VARIATION YOU MAY ALSO WISH TO ADD APPLES, RAISINS OR BLUEBERRIES TO PLAIN BATTER THEN TOP OFF WITH GLAZE OR GOODIES!

The Year I Lost My Smile

It was November 1998, and a few days before my birthday. And as always, the afternoon of my only day off would be filled with everything from cooking "crock pot stew" to children's chauffeur service. So naturally, while Bethany and I waited patiently for Michelle to get out of school, we were all certainly unprepared for what would nastily unfold next! See, once leaving the parking lot, we would drive off towards a busy intersection that would lead us back towards home. Then, moments later, I would be given the green-arrow advance to make a left turn from my lane. When suddenly, an elderly gentleman would attempt to turn my way as well from within his middle lane markers and next "entwined our bumpers together," making for a real mess on my passenger's side! Then, although it didn't take long for fifth-grade Bethany to wail "Mommy, there's a little old man stuck to the side of our car," we had bigger things to cope with. Sadly, I had just bumped my head on the driver's side door, causing my "just-done-at-the-dentist-after-months" teeth to throb, and my girls had some aches and pains too. But gratefully next, upon coming to a standstill, a few firefighters were able to free up our cars. Though, my goofy girlfriends would tease me much longer that there must be "a better way to secure a date then to snag some old goat in his eighties!" Yet, as humorous as that joke turned out to be, the horrible pain in my jaw wouldn't quit. Over time as well, I would be referred for Massage Therapy as a way to begin to lessen such hurt. Yet, while "Luke's" gifted touch was his greatest talent, it was his true stories that would mean even more. Knowingly too, he would also explain how our totally clenched-up bodies (after any accident) become so stressed by these sudden traumas, that it takes time to smooth out the kinks. Such would be the case also, with my persistent face pain, while eating my favorite softened strawberry ice cream made my mouth hurt so much worse.

Incredibly though, the more this "Master of Healing" and I grew together, I realized God had given me quite the gift. After all, Luke and I surely formed "a truly sacred bond" as we tried hard to save my three teeth. But, throughout these months of never smiling, he was sure to see I'd blush amidst a slew of "off-the-wall antics amidst his friends," most normal people would never admit! Then, around the same time, my step-mom, Lucy, would comment: "You really needed to slow down more, my dear, so now the Lord has made sure that you would." Besides, with each session I spent being healed by Luke's touch, I was enlightened beyond belief. As the more he manipulated my injuries, the more our pasts would fatefully merge! From comparing the woe-filled tales of such painful fathers and past relationships, to precious late relatives we'd both loved and lost, the more appointments we two would complete, the more like family we each would become.

Though one afternoon, after arriving for my weekly session, our tapestry-threaded bond would grow by leaps and bounds! Likewise, who would have thought that by Luke simply spotting my *You Are My Sunshine* key chain, framed within his soothing candlelight, would cause the depth of our discussions to soar to another level. And, talk about awesome comfort-quilt connections based on the magic of memories past! Here, Luke would tenderly share with me all about how "before his sick mother passed away when he was only nine, she would forever find the time to snuggle both her children and some cousins close while always singing *You Are My Sunshine* to them as well." Now, with each special memory that gushed that day, the more our hearts grasped the chance to air out. Remarkably too, a few-years-older Luke exemplified how he was ahead of me in experiencing that "God loves us even more in life when we make time to right our wrongs." At this time too, I was also busy *Life Is*

How YOU Look At It learning, to really lighten up! From this moment on, the weeks would just fly by while making it more than clear to me that my once-so-unlucky car accident had led to a place of higher peace. Above all, while Luke and I would always get a hearty laugh over his "leopard lovin' great aunts" and the opinions of my late Poppy, we knew we'd truly been given each other to accept EXACTLY who we both were!

A Blessing from the Bible

I always find "faith at my fingertips" whenever I read verses from my enlightening purple-covered Bible, which includes the following wonderfully worded passage about the Legacy of Love. Each time I leaf through my favorite book of I Corinthians, I am both reminded and assured that not only can love "move mountains" but it can also make for miracles!

Love

Though I speak with the tongues of men and of angels, but have not love, I have become sounding brass or a clanging cymbal.

And though I have the gift of prophecy, and understand all mysteries and all knowledge, and though I have all faith, so that I could remove mountains, but have not love, I am nothing.

And though I bestow all my goods to feed the poor, and though I give my body to be burned, but have not love, it profits me nothing.

Love suffers long and is kind; love does not envy; love does not parade itself, is not puffed up;

does not behave rudely, does not seek its own, is not provoked,

thinks no evil;

does not rejoice in iniquity, but rejoices in the truth;

bears all things, believes all things, hopes all things, endures all things.

Love never fails. But whether there are prophecies, they will fail; whether there are tongues, they will cease; whether there is knowledge, it will vanish away.

For we know in part and we prophesy in part.

But when that which is perfect has come, then that which is in part will be done away.

When I was a child, I spoke as a child, I understood as a child, I thought as a child; but when I became a man, I put away childish things.

For now we see in a mirror, dimly, but then face to face. Now I know in part, but then I shall know just as I am also known.

And now abide faith, hope, love, these three; but the greatest of these is love.

1 Corinthians 13: 1-13

"NKJV ™"

From Teddy Bears to Answered Prayers, When "Misfit" Met Her Match

"Jerri" was an unplanned child that her abusive father demanded his wife abort some forty-six years ago. But, her mom refused and brought her youngest daughter into the world anyway. Her childhood was horrible, as her alcoholic father was beyond cruel. Jerri always was on edge in her father's presence, as she never knew when he'd explode next. In fact, she was so nervous around her dad that she always made a mess at their dinner table while he scrutinized her every move. Once after spilling her drink, the rules forever changed. From that point on, she was forced to eat alone in another room. After this, her father only called her by "Misfit" and regularly told her how she was unlovable, while refusing himself also to ever acknowledge her real name. As a child, Jerri remembers going to school and observing how other parents kissed and hugged their children and took them on weekend picnics. Yet, there were no "warm-fuzzy" snuggles at her house, leaving Jerri aching for a way to feel wanted. Sadly too, when the bell rang at school on Friday afternoon, she and her siblings would cry as they dreaded any time spent around the house. Every weekend they would be whipped, no matter how hard they tried to behave. Somehow, Dad's whistle always blew or the porch light went on before they could make it home on time. Then, they were all in real trouble as their father found it oh-so-very funny to put them in their place!

Jerri's family lacked the traditional at-home luxuries, especially a car. Her father was self employed and only drove his pick-up truck. Holidays were unhappy also, as she rarely received surprises or any stylish clothes, settling for heartaches and hand-me-downs instead. As a young child, Jerri discovered love in her treasured teddy bears because they kept her "secrets and wouldn't yell back at her." Though, once her father was enlightened to this outlet of affection, he would set out to destroy her chances of receiving love from anything—even if it were just a stuffed animal. Here, he would take her cherished teddies and cut off their heads in front of her. Next, they would all be submerged in a bathtub of hot water where he would force Jerri to watch as he pretended to drown them. Later at night, her enabling mom would wring each water-logged little head out and sew them back onto their bodies. Over time, her teddy bears remained just as broken up as she was; though they continued to be her security blankets in life. Jerri also had pet dogs while growing up. They too, would provide steadfast warmth and soggy kisses without screaming at her. Yet, the fact that these faithful dogs would pay attention to her would fuel her father's anger even more—especially since they always growled in her defense any time that he would strike her. So, eventually, her dad took these beloved animals and dumped them off somewhere too, as something again was trying to love her. Meanwhile, her father would physically abuse her mother, while also having an affair with her aunt. In turn, the aunt would beat him for harming her sister. Finally, Jerri's mom had her husband arrested for spousal abuse, though in those days the police rarely stepped in. Woefully here, he served only eighteen days in jail at the time, returning with a real vengeance to wreak more havoc upon their AWFUL lives.

Then, at age thirteen, Jerri celebrated "What goes around comes around." As unexpectedly now, her father passed away leaving her to dance around the funeral home since her prayers had finally been heard! She was so relieved that this "horrible monster" would never be able to hurt her again. Wondrously next, her house was filled with a sense of peacefulness, while putting to rest the nightly ritual of drunken outbursts as well.

At the age of twenty-one, Jerri discovered a lump on the back of her neck which turned out to be malignant. Her doctors advised chemotherapy treatments three times a week for three months in a nearby, busy city. Here, she found herself traveling alone by cab, as no true family member could even be bothered to drive her. Here too, she entered a support group for those also "battling" cancer, sitting alone at every session as others would always arrive surrounded by lots of love. This scenario left Jerri both shy and scared, amidst some very painful childhood flashbacks also during this vulnerable time. Sadly now, she existed only as a hermit, retreating even deeper into her house of haunted thoughts. Furthermore, by feeling so unloved by a family poisoned by the ripple effects of abuse, she planned to stay a "single spinster" even after supremely beating this brutal cancer scare.

In her early forties, Jerri suffered with migraine headaches and some blackouts first thought to be stress-related by several of her doctors. Though, her actual diagnosis was much different. Once a bone scan was ordered, somehow to her sadness her dreaded cancer had returned. Now she would need both chemotherapy and radiation, while replacing her long brown locks instead with a mousy, light brown wig. At this point, she was also dealt the tragic suicide death of her younger brother—who was considered by all to be the favorite of the whole family. Likewise, she was truly heartbroken to know he'd left behind a wife and kids who would now grow old without him. Then, as Jerri bravely plugged along with her necessary treatments both her mom and aunt died within months of each other. Here, the untimely deaths of all of these loved ones not only left her wondering how life could be so cruel, but also constantly questioning what was in store for her next. Sadly, as she now nursed a gaping hole in her grieving heart, she also hoped at times that God would just let her give up too. It was here that her childhood connection to animals would be the only thing to save her, as she bonded with her new dog "Cocoa." Likewise, Jerri had rescued him as well from an abusive situation bringing him safely home to live with her and an older brother. (Where still today, Cocoa remains very sheepish around strangers due to his permanent hip injuries). Happily though, their unique thread of being "nobody's dog" and "nobody's daughter" has resulted in a solid bond that neither will abandon the other, as lots of shared kisses and comfort now rule over loneliness and limps!

When "Misfit" Met Her Match—Part II

In late 1997, Jerri was introduced to "Sam," both a dear friend of her older brother and no stranger to heartache either. Years ago, after losing his alcoholic father to the "battle of the bottle," he headed off to Florida to clean up his act as well. While feeling less-than-lucky in the love department after several roller-coaster relationships, Sam also was sworn to singlehood. But, after one such outburst with his ex-girlfriend, he would be spending the night at Jerri's house at the invitation of her big brother. And, at first glance, she didn't really like him. Yet, she had a sudden change of heart when she saw him sleeping the next morning . . . with his new "companion." Here, Sam's arms were now wrapped around her childhood stuffed tiger that had surely fallen from atop the couch, while keeping it close to his heart. This tender moment unveiled to Jerri her two favorite traits in any man—he was an animal lover and a "cuddler!" Then, from this day on, Sam often asked to date her, but Jerri boldly refused. Woefully, her ongoing cancer fight had left her feeling unattractive in anyone's eyes including those of her wanna-be man. But, in 1998, her cancer went into remission—allowing Jerri to believe she was now "enough of a genuine woman" to give dating Sam a chance. Besides, she now saw Sam through softer eyes, as she no longer felt like a burden.

Unlike previous holidays, New Years Eve would be wonderful! As Jerri and her "knight" danced every dance, she treasured most his precious gifts of passionate kisses and promises kept. Though, once the party was all wrapped up,

Sam invited Jerri back to spend the night at his place. Yet, while not wanting to rush things, she politely declined and drove herself home instead.

The next afternoon, when Sam returned to Jerri's house he brought a surprise from his mom, "Esther." It was a special jar of homemade jelly that truly warmed her heart. However, Jerri was most grateful for the times that Sam would hold her tenderly and would tell anyone within earshot how, "He treats me just like gold." Moreover, Sam's family had also grown to accept and adore her. I should know, as Sam is "my girlfriend Denise's" big brother and they've adopted me too! Furthermore, I liked Jerri from the moment that I met her. Together too, we've shared the bliss of girlish giggles while also "fighting" over the bowl of Esther's unbelievable steamed carrots! Yet, ever present in the kitchen was a wonderful aura that these two belonged together, as an "undeniable warmth" appeared each time we were in their presence.

During the summer of 1998, a new bone scan showed Jerri's cancer had returned. While sadly running rampant, her doctors now shared too, how she had only about six months to live. Next, she began a series of blood transfusions in an effort to keep up her strength. Yet, above all, my special "older sister" maintained an upbeat attitude while regularly stating how she never "felt that sick."

Little did I know that on Christmas Day 1999 I would once again be reminded how "delicious" it feels to immerse myself in those who truly love me the most. See, after exchanging gifts with another friend and dropping my girls off at Grandma's, I was driving to dinner at Denise's house where I always fit right in. Once in the driveway, I picked up my new candle threesome and read the calligraphy on each of the frosted jars, "Love," "Friendship" and "Caring," before sliding them into my purse. Lastly, I scurried up the steps, hoping I hadn't missed much of the festivities. Though as I walked into the living room, I was just in time to observe how true love can cause miracles! Where, from a chair in the corner, Jerri was busy opening her Christmas gifts with the excitement of an eight-year-old! As she eagerly peered into the box on her lap, she lifted out a little piece of wood that Sam claimed to have "borrowed" from their backyard. Next, while digging a little deeper, Jerri discovered a tiny box that she surmised out loud was a new pair of earrings. But, upon sweetly opening her new jeweled treasure, she was beyond shocked! Now, as this woman once known as Misfit displayed a "Woo-Hoo" diamond ring, Sam got down on one knee and proposed! Moreover, the magic in the room was so overwhelming, as realistically our much-loved angel had only a few weeks to live. So, at this point, I reached into my purse and removed the red "Love" candle from its wrapper, while making them both promise me to "keep it burning brightly" wherever their journey may lead. Once seated around the kitchen table, Jerri and I naturally "sparred off" again as we'd sweetly been reacquainted with how we are never too old for surprises! While assuming each Christmas that there would always be room for Esther's homemade carrots, we'd forgotten about those exquisite "heartfelt carats"—as Jerri's newly decorated ring finger now sparkled as much as her non-stop smile!

Shortly thereafter, this couple's time was cut short as Jerri ended up in the Intensive Care, delaying their wedding date as well. Then, in the months ahead, another bone scan was ordered resulting in absolutely no traces of cancer anywhere. Therefore, Jerri is felt by her doctors to be a precious "medical miracle" based on the positive combination of her thinking, her treatments and her trust in God!

In September of 2000, they were finally married. Though prior to the ceremony, Jerri recalls waiting with nervous anticipation for the arrival of their two family limousines. Now, as her knees knocked with fright, her mind reflected back to "the pain of her past." At this juncture, she also vividly recalled how anything sh'd ever dared to love had always deserted her in life. Yet, minutes later, the first car arrived carrying her much-loved in-laws-to-be. Sweetly here, Jerri's focus instantly shifted from those "left over feelings" she had stuffed deep inside—to love, nuptials and happiness on her day as a bride! And, as Sam arrived shortly thereafter in limo number two he proudly took his place, faithfully standing beside her not fearfully standing her up.

When "Misfit" Met Her Match—Part III

Last summer, I joined these two newlyweds for a first-time visit to their house after accepting an invite to dinner. With a spring in my step, I came totally prepared with a pen and a pad of paper. And, just like Jerri's smile on that mind-blowing Christmas, I could hardly wait to scribble this romance as part of my sacred memoirs. Upon entering that once-scary house, I felt so right at home. Even their dog "Cocoa," normally afraid of strangers, covered my cheeks in kisses! Then, Jerri began to tell her side of the story (at the same kitchen table where she is "allowed" to sit today!) as Sam retreated to the living room to relax with the remote. Then, once jotting down Jerri's magical account our conversation shifted to "the message" of my book. At this point, I enlightened her to my "Tapestry Theory" that we are all sacredly tied together by our cherished encounters (like children, conversations and colors) which help us to shed some healthy light upon the subjects we most need to heal. And, by paying attention to those things we attract truly only "once we're spiritually ready," our life's stress load becomes much lighter by letting the less than perfect go. Likewise, I further explained that while doing the internal audit to heal these tough times, we can conquer our feelings of "sadness and shame" by focusing instead on the love of our Saving Graces. These Godsends, being our own "Angels on Earth," are the people, places and patchwork that make the low times bearable. And, by consciously dragging around this "comfort quilt," we are constantly reminded to reminisce and recharge. Happily as well, by harvesting the gifts within our intuition, we become enlightened, while optimally given the true clarity to keep our heads held high.

Now, as an example here, I tossed out to Jerri that my own favorite "tapestry thread" was my childhood Cinderella watch, a precious link from my fuzzy past. See, this treasured timepiece was given to me in grade school by my Mom during the days when (to me) we felt like a family. When suddenly I was amazed how "just simply voicing our true vulnerability" strikes a chord in the heartstrings of those we are conversing with! Next, Jerri's eyes lit up, as she too was the proud owner of a genuine Cinderella watch, which was a special gift from her late mother and stored in a jewelry box somewhere! Incredibly, I could barely contain my excitement as she invited me upstairs to get a glimpse of our happiest heirloom (as I remember being heartbroken when my "princess watch" no longer worked and so-sadly bit the dust). Now, we raced up the steps, two-at a time, as the eight-year-olds we had suddenly become. Though, halfway up the stairs while savoring the moment, I truly saw that my Tapestry Theory was truly right on target! Sweetly, Jerri's pre-adult passions were still alive and well, as witnessed by an array of stuffed animals and glistening angels galore! More amazing to me though, was the unexpected surprise I encountered when she switched on the bedroom light. You see, forever framing the large wooden windows in her age forty-something room appeared some timeless teddy bear curtains! Lastly, as we searched through her closet, we were unable to locate Jerri's Cinderella keepsake. But, as the loving sisters we'd eternally become, we would forever wallow in the bond of such a beautifully moving connection.

Once returning downstairs, it was Sam's turn to tell his tale. Though, when I sat down next to him, I couldn't help but question "What was it about meeting Jerri that could possibly make this once hardened-by-heartache man gravitate from a non-committal guy, to a newly-married groom in only a matter of months?" Especially since he had proposed to the love of his life as her stay on this Earth was expected to be short and sweet? His quick answer brought tears to my eyes as he stated without hesitation, "I didn't care if we had two months or two years together, I just knew in my heart that I had to be with her. She's my best friend, as we lean on each other in good and bad times, and money does not matter." Here also, they both divulged their secret for keeping their relationship intact. Quality couple time sealed with especially cherished kisses!

Yet, even more remarkable was the gift that these "two lovebirds" unveiled before my eyes. See, in order to fulfill my favorite fairy-tale ending of "living happily-ever-after," I too need to push past my fear of ever falling in love again. And, although I've been labeled selectively single over the years, I can relate more to being "scared shitless" of any continued heartache and hurt. Then recently, while looking in the bathroom mirror, I discovered that the flashing neon sign once scrawled across my forehead stating "off limits and unlovable" had surely disappeared! At this point too, I knew, that no one else could possibly have loved me until I *Life Is How YOU Look At It* learned that I was worthy of being loved.

Meanwhile, when Thanksgiving time came, I was blessed with "several signs" that I am on the right track when it comes to really reviving romance. See, I spent the holiday itself with the other side of Denise's family, where last year this foursome lost everything they owned in one twenty-minute fire. Next, as we toured this newly built house, we all marveled at those things usually taken for granted—like family, faith and furnishings. Then, upon entering the living room, the glow of the flickering fireplace sent an unexpected surge of warmth straight to my soul! My, how I too had missed "making memories while sipping hot chocolate in front of a crackling fire, complete with a tender partner's 'pillow talk' into the early hours of the dawn."

Yet tonight, two days after Thanksgiving, we're all heading over to Esther's house for another holiday happening. Once again, I can hardly wait to see Jerri as I have a surprise for her. A few weeks ago, while whimsically "treasure hunting," I discovered a genuine tapestry-threaded tidbit that had her name written all over it! Wondrously, it's an adult-sized denim shirt covered in the comfort of cute teddy bears. And, when I saw it I just knew that Jerri had to have it as sometimes those old hand-me-downs still have a way of giving us hope.

This year, Thanksgiving to me was more about addressing my strongest fears. After all, "Life surely isn't celebrated by those who sit on the sidelines!" Then, recently while meditating, I "also released to the universe" the two cherished issues closest to my heart while knowing they will find their way back only when fate sees fit. First off, I have prayed for the speedy rediscovery of my childhood Cinderella watch as I continue to search the antique stores for it. Second, I've wished for the spirit of my Soul Mate to light up my life with his sunshine and stability. Meanwhile, I can almost hear

Poppy raising "hoopla in heaven," as he'd always hoped for the day I'd miraculously want to settle down again. Yet, until that date with destiny, I will continue to explore my own "commitment vs. cohabitation" fears, while knowing my next "prince" will need to be as patient as he is passionate! Though, the biggest lesson I have learned in seeing Sam and Jerri positively prevail is that, "loving again, while healing our hearts, can make for all-out miracles." Moreover, since no obstacle is ever too enormous to overcome, we all have the abundant option to live out our lives in love.

AND, TODAY I TRULY BELIEVE . . .

No matter how much in life we've loved
and lost, or "been injured" throughout times
in our past, we can believe in the power of passion
and prayers—as sometimes God saves the
BEST love for last!

How Jerri "Did It Her Way"

As spring approached, Jerri would find her once so-gutsy stamina seriously going downhill. As sadly, somewhere between all the treatments and transfusions, her body had been through enough. Once May arrived, her spirit as well was starting to succumb. And, while we would still all meet less often for dinner, we knew the Lord's "warmly beckoning light" would soon be making other plans. Then, it was almost June when that dreaded call came as I was sitting at my Emergency Room desk. And, while Jerri predominantly "wandered in and out of this world," my family would keep me posted. Though next, I found I was not only giving star-spangled service to those sitting across from me, but was hurting as much on the inside as the ones I was supposed to help soothe! When suddenly, it occurred to me how I'd be "of no good to anyone else that day if I didn't make family come first." After all, if the shoe were on the other foot, sweet Jerri would never have had to think twice. Then, I did something even short of a miracle when I called up my boss and shared that I had to leave. Now, within minutes, another coworker arrived leaving me free to tell my "slipping sister" how much she was actually loved! Meanwhile, as I made the half-hour drive to her hometown hospital, I prayed that God would just "keep her a little bit longer" on His so-awesome Earth. Incredibly too, I couldn't help but smile as my mind mulled over her truly brazen antics of the past few days. Furthermore, who besides Jerri could arise from an ICU bed, abruptly cancel her DNR order, and then spend two glorious days parading around in the sun with her carefree prince and childlike pets? Yet, right after this blissful encounter, she would find herself right back upon death's door. But, this time, upon entering the Critical Care area I just knew by my "millions of churning butterflies" that I'd be leaving my loved one behind. Once inside Jerri's tube-filled room, she would tenderly grasp my hand. And, as our "tapestry threads" entwined again with lots of unconditional love, she made me promise her two things. The first was to seriously publish these works, and the second to watch over Sam. Then, moments later, her "life's candle" would cease; though I had become a better person just by having known her.

On the tear-filled ride home, I couldn't help but notice how I was managing to "hit" every red light on the road. Yet, making this situation worse was the fact that the summer sun was beginning to settle in a series of streaks too bright for my sunglasses. So, with every stop, I would allow myself to mindfully savor the vibrant spirit of Jerri. Next, I vividly recalled when I was writing her story, how I'd finally secured "that lovely Corinthians verse" (with the perfectly worded "mirror part") in none other than my purple-covered Bible! Then, at the next stoplight, I *Life Is How YOU Look At It* saw how it is truly possible to end up a "blessed little sister" when I had only been born the big! Somehow too, Jerri would always take it upon herself to out-do any surprises I did! Sadly too, this "Misfit" who'd come to mean so much was surely going to be missed.

Now, with only a few stoplights left to go, I was in for quite a shock! See, the pending sunset had altered itself into a blitz of pastel colors, covering like billows of cotton candy every inch of the evening sky! And, while seeming to resemble a Fourth of July finale, I could not help but admire Jerri's genuine uniqueness. After all, she may have been labeled "that unwanted child" years ago, but would have womanly wanted to "go out with a bang!" Then, once arriving at home, I would find solace in our cherished "tapestry threads" as I wrapped myself up in the "red roses" sweater she'd given, and curled up with Corinthians love.

The next afternoon would be a tough one, as I needed to both select Jerri's flowers and find something quick to wear. Yet, once inside the florist's shop, this tear-filled effort would be easier than I thought. As suddenly, in warm memory of Jerri while leafing through shiny pages, "one sparkling display" marked her light through the ages! Then, when I walked towards the counter to locate some staff, the truly perfect "animal accent" was peering back at me. Here, as I picked up this satin teddy bear done up in warm pastels, I knew this "little Misfit" had surely found himself a home right in the middle of Jerri's so-magical arrangement! Moreover, it was hard to be sad about losing sweet Jerri, as she'd actually lived, I felt three years longer to show me again to love.

The following day would be her funeral, where I would get to chat with her never-met pal. And, while Jerri appeared every part of a lady, "Helen" was finding it hard to cope without her best friend's "signature, sweet finesse." Then minutes later, funeral services would start as the minister walked up to the front. Yet, what was said now as she celebrated Jerri's spectacular spirit would send a comforting rush of chills up my spine! Moreover, when she first began preaching from "Love is patient Love is kind . . ." to the crowd, I practically fell off my seat. Next, she would make mention of Jerri's loving family, first about a devoted husband, then her two faithful dogs—which she always thought of as "her kids." As this eulogy went on, she would attempt to subdue the raw ache in us all by telling everyone to simply remember those special tapestry threads that together we would each always share. Finally, it was time for "the family" to bid Jerri a final farewell. Here, I would grasp a weeping Helen's hand and help her walk up to the front. Where suddenly, as we headed past the flowers to exit, I knew exactly how to help! After all, Helen may have lost her best friend, but I could bestow upon her the next best thing. With this thought in mind, I plucked that warm and fuzzy teddy bear from its post within the flowers, and asked Helen to please take him home. Besides, our Jerri was too much of an "avid princess" to allow anyone she loved to feel pain.

About one year later, I'd be off to the toy store with Bethany (which now only her mother allowably calls her) to pick out a new BMX bike. And, while she could barely contain her excitement, she'd already found the one she liked best after walking the mall with some friends. So once inside, an employee would have to remove this silver bicycle from within the ceiling-high racks. As he placed this soon-to-be purchase in front of our feet, I could not believe my eyes! Sweetly, detailed on the frame of Bethany's well-earned hafta-have was none other than the huge word "MISFIT," causing each of us to crack a bittersweet smile amidst holding back our tears. Here also, I couldn't help but think how "Sometimes losing someone is not the end of the world, but makes way for more love to move in!" Besides, their many comfort quilt—connections don't cease just because they have moved on. That night too, while pouring the magic of this "ah-ha moment" out onto thirsty paper, I had three more *Life Is How YOU Look At It* rumbling revelations. First, we should all be forced at times to "sit the other side of our desks" to see exactly the kind of service we are giving! Second, those old hand-me-downs of unwanted things not only give us hope, but truly help us to heal. Lastly, there is a little "Misfit" in each of us just waiting to be hugged, held or heard. Though the luckiest of these treasured beings are those who develop the true "silver linings" amidst the heavy hands they were once dealt!

"Before your dreams can come true, you have to have those dreams."

~ Dr. Joyce Brothers

The Magic of "My Michael's"— How Time Truly Heals All Wounds

Early on in my awakening, I was enlightened to the presence of "Heavenly Angel guides." After eagerly researching the four archangels: Michael, Raphael, Gabriel and Uriel, I cherished most how "these cherubs" were always mine for-the-mention! At this point of my studies, I was expected to figure out which of the four wonders was truly my Guardian Angel to no longer just sit on my shoulder in support, but to shine his light brightly on all I could be. Next, I completed a survey on statistics that made me special, like my birthday, background and beliefs. Once combining these results with a soothing round of meditation, the warmth of "Michael's magic" found its way home to my heart. While sometimes appearing in a suit of armor sporting a sword in one hand and a scale in another, this shiny saint portrays a mix of balance and beauty. (And, humorously showing also, how it is possible to "have a man in my life" even if my girlfriends can't see him!) Miraculously too, once I learned to tune into God's manifested gift of my own "angelic tendencies," I watched my treasured dreams turn slowly into truths after mixing them with the reality of making my needs known.

Somehow, it's still the men named "Michael" who seemingly have the most to teach me about honesty, healing and happiness; while patiently proving as well that all angels aren't invisible and may appear right out of the blue! Awesomely, these wonders who continue to show me the way have been both a "blessed windfall" of softness and strength at times when I've summoned them most! Amidst forever clad in an armor of protection and positive thinking, they have bravely chosen to stand beside me, especially during the days when I "dug down deep and dealt with my darkness amidst grappling with my grief." Though, it was during these times as I wrestled with my own inner ugliness that I truly appeared most beautiful in their understanding eyes. Incredibly, by rediscovering beachfront fun again as a "teenager," facing my abuse-laden traumas which had begun to flourish in my late thirties and finally, by enlightening me how "being open and honest with others does not always end in heartache"—I too, have earned my wings! Meanwhile, as "all my Michael's" make for sweet memories, I have been shown also that real men don't desert me in times more full of sadness than full of sun! And, foremost, once trading "painful past realities" for passionate present rainbows, I saw my life's reflection in a whole new revealing light.

Yet, never has their angelic assistance been more appreciated by my awakened "inner child" then during December 2001's holiday season and my dream-come-true date with destiny. Here, one of my Michael's was coming to town for a pre-Christmas shop-fest and to help out with some handy work. Happily, with each time we reconnect, he continues to teach me how "loving and losing isn't necessarily a negative, but proof-positive that I deserve more." Therefore, I'm proud to pen that true gentleman still exist, as it is possible to ask and be acknowledged, stay close friends without "hitting the pillows," and be allowably honest as we engage in those keepsake conversations that reveal the stuff that dreams are made of. And, on this winter day, we were both in luck as Michael carefully selected his Christmas cards and an illuminated angel to top off my tree. Then together, we discovered that perfectly worded now purple-covered Bible to make Misfit's memoir complete! Once back at my house, and after enjoying some Chinese take-out, Michael got busy tinkering with his tool belt. Next, I began to share some of my favorite writings with him, by excitedly reading from the corner of the couch, while his calming nature easily boosted my confidence. Meanwhile, as I choked up on the ending to "How Misfit Met Her Match," he'd just wrapped up his workload making it almost time to call it a night. Amidst holding my breath I awaited his heartfelt reaction, figuring he would find my scripted style either "too mushy" for a guy or totally-to-him miraculous. Now, to my sweet surprise, our conversation deepened while we took off on several tangents of some tender-to-us topics. As we openly covered everything from "our fears of getting hurt again, forever completing our cherished clock collections, and my eight-year antique store search to bring that childhood Cinderella watch home to my heart"—I truly lavished the fact that real angels love to listen! Finally, as darkness deeply descended, Michael was ready to return home. Likewise, after exchanging quick hugs in the hallway, he headed out into the snow and I swiftly "hibernated" to my kitchen to begin to write some more. Here also, I was forever changed, once merging head-on with Michael's awesome spirit and sweetly *Life Is How YOU Look At It* learning, how "trusting again" is a two-way street. Suddenly, it dawned on me to alter my set-in-stone plan and now write from a slant, reaching "both sensitive sexes" to hopefully appeal to anyone (like me), who's truly been touched by an angel!

Then, about three weeks after Christmas, Michael called to invite me out for dinner, while also wishing to spend some time and spoil me. Though, while he already knew I'd promised to write religiously throughout the winter; we both

agreed it would do me good to "come out from the convent"
for some Sunday evening fun. When that day arrived, we
found ourselves at Swiss Chalet for some chicken dinners;
the perfect place to be on a very rainy night. After indulging
in the warmth of comfort foods and cozy conversation, I
was once again enlightened as to how our time together
truly flies. See, as usual, our conversation "clicked" and now
centered around our out-of-town best friends" who are not
only married to each other, but were doing their best to fix
us up. Yet tonight at the table, this very special man had
so much more on his plate. As midway through our main
course, Michael mindfully mentioned "the unbelievable
impact my previously read-aloud stories had in jarring his
own memories" (while also pointing out perfectly that we are
never too old to bring our "soft spots" to the surface amidst
those we truly believe in). Meanwhile, as he continued to
tell his tale, he spoke of a really close friend who'd collected
clocks and watches right along with him. About eight years
ago, as this much-admired man lay dying, he gifted this
sweet Michael with two treasured timepieces which this
"unforeseen angel" had safely tucked away for such a rainy
day! He further explained that it was not until he'd heard me
pray for the safe return of my childhood Cinderella watch,
would he leave my house that snowy night remembering that
he, too, owned a princess watch though unsure of just which

one. It was at this moment, when he reached into his right coat pocket, that I was shocked to discover how fairy tales can come true at any age if we risk exposing our dreams to daylight. Where next, when Michael placed my "home-at last heirloom" gently into my left hand, Cinderella's charm truly glowed as much as I had remembered! And, as tender childhood tears of thankfulness trickled down my cheeks, I too, felt like a rediscovered princess. At this point, my thoughts traveled back to that tapestry-threaded night when I was reading to Michael amidst all of his repairs. Above all, I'd been blessed beyond belief for making the conscious choice to share "Misfit's story" with him. Especially since I had almost nixed the idea as it was seemingly getting late. Even more amazing though, was the fact that Michael had kept this precious patchwork from my past for about eight total years—the same amount of time I'd been combing the antique stores for it. Miraculously, he had never gifted this watch as well, to either of his two grown daughters!

Today, I continue to be the recipient of never taken-for-granted nudges from my own Guardian Angels, who truly walk on water in my eyes. As they spiritually provide me with "a beautiful balance of both lighting up my life and lightening my load," I no longer feel lost in a "shuffle of shoulds." And, just like Jerri, I too have been reacquainted with the concept of being treated just like gold. Likewise, after "strongly sensing" that each of them has been heaven-sent by Poppy to both blanket and believe in me, I can still feel my grandfather's same wondrous warmth in the beauty of their beings. Finally, amidst the spontaneity and sunshine, each of "my Michael's" gratefully provide the reality forever remains that the giddy eight-year-olds in all of us are never too old for a great game of Gotcha last!

The Magic of My Michael's Part II —On Life, Love and Promising The Doves!

As I was putting the finishing touches on this exact paragraph, I was "sent several signs" that I'm right where I am supposed to be. Incredibly, it is the morning before Easter 2002, and as the sunlight caressed my covers, I was suddenly awakened by a "soothing stream of thankful thoughts" running through my mind. Moreover, I sweetly reflected upon the non-stop gifts of rebirth and renewal, amongst the eternally "never-can-acquire-enough angels" motto in my life. Here too, I found myself cherishing most the comfort of Christ in my corner, as it is supremely HIS Love that "Lets there be light" as I become ready to reach out (not retreat from) the returning "rainbow of romance." Next, during this eye-opening vision, my thoughts traveled back to attending the musical *Jesus Christ Superstar* as a teenager. Here, Mary Magdalene sang about her vulnerability about expressing her love for Jesus. In her solo entitled *I Don't Know How To Love Him,* she portrays beautifully how we all need to balance both the softness and strength that we exhibit our beloved, by not always having the answers, but daring to do it all anyway. Therefore, by simply "blitzing our negative fears" with the utmost of faith and forgiveness, we too, will set the stage for a fresh start. Yet even more important, after making peace with our past's baggage to purposefully live in the moment, we institute our own "outer boundaries" which ensures the ultimate of awareness without leaving us bogged down. Also, by establishing a solid "priorities program" (as my Michael's have proven perfectly), precious time-outs can still be taken from whatever the world sends our way! And, as this pre-Easter vision continued to illuminate, I sleepily pondered the sweet return of my Cinderella watch home to my heart so quickly. Meanwhile, amongst the radiant sun rays, I was magically made aware that I'm certainly one step closer to meeting my own "knight in shining armor"—even as my misted cloud cover seems to be raining the wrong men! But intuitively also, I must keep my personal promise to punctually complete my callings. First, by searching inward to ensure optimal fulfillment, then by scribbling these *Life Is How YOU Look At It* pages for all the world to see. Likewise, about a week prior to this revelation, I'd prayed to God whether to diligently pursue my love of book writing or to dive back into the dating pool—since everyone but me was having a tough time liking my limits!

To my amazement, as this morning of miracles further unfolded, a live single dove suddenly appeared outside my bedroom window (while making sure to foil any chances of me ever falling back to sleep!) At this point, I happily remembered how a pair of devoted love doves had faithfully occupied Poppy's purple lilac bush behind my house for years! Remarkably here, I must've heard my grandfather tell me a million times how "these kindred spirits mate for life" as rarely seen without the one who makes their heart complete. Though, this unexpected bird was busy trying to tell me exactly what I already knew. For now, I too, must follow in fate's footsteps. See, as only by being fulfilled can I bring fulfillment to another and live wholesomely ever after! Yet, before that day arrives, just like my comforting "cooing dove soul sister," I shall be content to appreciate the miracles in each moment alone—until the magic of my spiritual Godsend arrives home to mesh with my mending heart. Though foremost, I've learned that by doing the dirty work to release my own "armor of abuse," my soul now sings as well after experiencing the new-found freedom that loving all my facets provides. Somehow too, while rediscovering my teenage-like innocence to face my fears as if loving for the very first time, the stage is now set for attracting the right relationship. Furthermore, my new focus is warmly one that won't end up with the "rug of trust" being ripped out from under me, but may very well be, sweet renewed faith in the magic carpet ride of a lifetime.

Here also, I can't help but smile when I think back to how my Poppy would forever tease me that "The next man in your life certainly has his work cut out for him, Missy." (Though he never did live long enough to know that I've been busy also growing into a new-and-improved piece of work!) Besides, while having survived enough warfare to know that I won't settle for anything less than "a passionate gentleman to properly grow old with," my mirroring prince will be well worth the wait; though he'll need to treat me tenderly as "my Michael's" will be watching. And, once regally bound together by our faith-first beliefs, this reality will find us planting our own precious garden of balance and beauty—one surely rich in romance, roses and respect. Finally, though never taking for granted the love of this one-in-a-million man amidst a "forever-grateful backdrop" of honesty, healing and happiness; enriching his precious spirit shall remain more priceless to my heartstrings than any pile of possessions ever could!

*** For my readers:

*   Can you think of any angels in your life who have seemingly appeared out of nowhere?
*   Are you a believer too, in true angels amongst us on Earth?
*   Do you think of that "special someone" in the words of a favorite song or fragrant scent?

The Poem That Wouldn't Leave Me Alone

Early one morning in February 1998, I was awakened from a deep sleep. Stirring around inside of me was a wave of mixed emotions too strong to deny. So strong, that I actually called in sick that morning to try and make sense of them all! With more "inner prompting", I pulled out a pen and rapidly began to scribble some thoughts. And, six pages later, I was really proud of my finished piece! Besides, I had always loved to write poetry, leaving me thankful as an adult that I had not lost my touch for the tender. Yet, while also examining all I'd just written, I would be in for quite a surprise. By reviewing these newly surfaced feelings that I had just poured out on paper, I found they all had a similar theme. One of taken-by-me travels I'd surely somehow suppressed! While my first poem version appeared very "sugar-coated," it also featured others whom had both loved and left me in life. At the same time, my special memories about each person were "connected to a sacred color" that, when all combined together, formed a rainbow unlike any other! See, from sipping "poiple" grape juice with my dad (yes, I also had a speech impediment), to wearing a Cinderella-blue prom gown, my once-faded but glitzy flashbacks were filled with smiles and softness galore. Though, as this enlightening morning progressed, I was again moved to pick up that very enlightening pen. Only this time, after I'd finished with my "flurry of the forgotten," I was left staring at about ten pages that weren't too pretty on paper. To my sudden disgust, amidst all the real people, real memories and rainbow-themed backdrop; I discovered myself to be an ongoing participant to "the tapestry thread of abuse." Now, as these sordid memories next unveiled, I was that little girl left behind in the car while the others would bring me back some ice cream, since my overbite was (as explained by an adult) "just too ugly to be seen in public." Then, I recalled being that "trusting pre-teen all alone with a relative" whose phoned invitation for magic and music turned into raw incest, as I could not pry myself free from his grip. Then, as these once-fuzzy episodes progressed onward to my teenage years, even the role of "family scapegoat" I'd landed still felt so unworthy and unloved. Furthermore, it began to make sense to me why I had been wrongly labeled "promiscuous" by once-adoring relatives from here to Pennsylvania, by another so painfully-at-times jealous that she just had to make things up. Furthermore, the heart-wrenching repercussions of always being in the "right place at the wrong time" would continue to haunt me, especially at home.

As time progressed further, I pretty much evolved as well into a "childhood Cinderella," with too much hafta-do's and homework for any twelve-year-old to take on. So, once growing old enough to leave this house, I would next be raped by someone I'd trusted, only to solicit that elder one's aid again and not to be believed. Moreover, while still dressed amidst the soiled clothes from the previous night's shameful outcome, I was told sternly to keep quiet or risk being "locked up in the mental ward" where I would lose my little girl. Yet foremost here, once "firmly back" into my age thirty-something skin, my badly trembling body felt like I had just been blitzed by an emotionally-filled snowball war with none to throw back from my side! Though, at this crushing moment with all of my history oozing out in the open, I intuitively knew that I still had a choice. I could explore these feelings in therapy, find some new friends and attempt to "figure out me;" or stay shell-shocked in all I'd just learned! So, on this chilly February morning, I made a *Life Is How YOU Look at It* promise to myself. I was going to review every line in that poem and begin to purge all the hurt. Besides, I did not have to keep reliving "these traumas," but was determined to reveal the truth! Lastly, as nightfall slowly descended, I boxed my eye-opening poem under the bed for safekeeping and was somehow thankful to have seen the light.

A few weeks later, I would once again be led to lift the lid off that "shadowed box." Though as scary as this action became through the months, it was so much easier than just staying stuck! Then, excitedly from out of the woodwork, other "vessels" would appear—validating everything from the beauty of precious Amethyst rocks to publicly bearing witness, as well, to other once hushed-up affairs. Yet, here too, like that really injured monarch butterfly had blissfully taught me the "more weighted worries" I was able to release, the lighter my wings would become!

Shortly thereafter, when I mentioned "The Poem That Wouldn't Leave Me Alone" and it's obviously spiritual origin to one of my friends, she seemed to find this all too amusing. First off, she would now explain, how "we each have our life-changing stories to tell." Yet, the fear of other's opinions keeps us from doing our real life's work. Here, as I next joked to "Fifi" how my free-flowing writings sometimes felt, like I was "hanging my most-skimpiest of underwear out on the clothesline for all of the world to see" she once again giggled as though she understood. Moreover, as time has progressed onward, I've had a real change of heart. Although Fifi may have admittedly tried to burst my book-writing bubble, I have become more determined than ever to beat those ugly odds. Besides, maybe life is meant to focus less on our *Life Is How YOU Look At It*, self-defeating behaviors (like abandonment issues and underwear insights) and instead, celebrate firmly the wonders of our own awe! Yet, in the end, while it always helps to forgive a "friend" who will forever sabotage it as she sees it—I can't help but think as my once-buried thoughts burst out onto porous paper; what better investment is there then to invest back into ourselves?

*** More reflection upon my preface to "The Poem That Wouldn't Leave Me Alone"

While meditating recently, I saw two white doves and a flickering red candle, followed brilliantly by a large, sky-stretching rainbow with a pot of gold at the end. And, although it has seemed like forever to decipher these "fateful meanings," this hope-laden poem has healed both my life and my broken heart.

From "Rindercella" to Reality

About three years ago, I would be meeting my sweet friend Dana out for some overdue lunch. Upon arriving at our secluded spot, I couldn't help but notice how "something" had certainly brightened her spirit. This happy woman went on to explain how, with the help of "a Native American lady, she had done some inner healing" which would both cleanse her heart and caress her re-born soul. Wondrously too, she had learned to forgive her rapist (which had also years ago resulted in the birth of her first-born son), while giving her back "the uplifting freedom" to shine loads more light upon who SHE was! Foremost, Dana was the perfect example of how healing incredibly happens from the inside out! Suddenly here, I wasn't half as interested in eating our subs as I was in her huge success. At the same time, I would explain to her that my book writing journey had seemingly been at a standstill, while I eagerly awaited the next spiritual clue. Yet, this mission hadn't been easy on me either. From being born first on Mickey Mouse's birthday, to now becoming a maiden "inspirational beacon" to other miracles in need. Next, Dana would explain how she'd worked so hard with this remarkable woman, who would make her life less stressful by accompanying her to again revisit, some traumatic, though unhealed scenes. Amazingly too, while pursuing this adventure from a now-adult perspective, she also found her "passionate power" had returned, as these once-fuzzy pieces timely fell into place. So you can only imagine my surprise to learn how this wonder's name was "Minnie." Surely another comfort quilt connection I was more-than-meant to pursue. Therefore, before leaving behind our lunch, I'd be given this woman's number; though it would take me several days myself to summon up the courage to even give her a call. Meanwhile, during the weeks before my September 12th appointment (also my deceased friend, Diane's, birthday), many strange occurrences began to happen to me. Almost overnight, those fire alarms with strobe lights at work had begun to give me headaches. Then, the rank smells of beer and coffee anywhere around kept me beyond nauseous—and I encountered a basket of rosary beads (forever placed by our hospital's chapel), that when I picked up the purple ones, chills ran down my spine. Moreover, the more these "tapestry threads" kept repeating, the more I kept wondering what had really gone wrong! At the same time, Minnie phoned me with some very explicit instructions. To wear only my own jeans and jewelry, to eat a very light breakfast that morning, and to please come prepared with some crayons and colored pencils to help her talents to start to heal me.

Though once that day arrived, and I was seated at Minnie's table, her mood would suddenly change. It was here that she would enlighten me how she "never deals with anyone but her Native American kind." Meanwhile, I knew I hadn't come this far in my remarkable journey not to set the record straight! Now, I would swiftly point out to Minnie how her intuitive culture had made up a major part of my Life Lessons, from observing a refreshed Dana, to my enlightening step mom Lucy to my lucky-to-have middle name. I also explained further how this whole fateful experience seriously paralleled "mindfully being in childbirth labor," as the more I kept uncovering the more I wanted to push! Next, as the kitchen fell silent, I silently prayed for my cherished cause to continue along. Seconds later, I'd also convey to Minnie how I was in the midst of a book writing mission, having been "sent amidst her expertise" to reveal more pages to write. Then, as several minutes passed, she would agree to take me on as a client, but only if I was willing to do every inch of the grueling work. And, while not really knowing what I was getting myself into, I trusted wholly in mirrored divinity and my dearest Dana to know this trip was meant to be. So, my search for the truth would begin . . .

From "Rindercella" to Reality—Part II

During our first visit, Minnie would start to give me a series of artwork instructions, when suddenly she would need to stop dead within her tracks! She would next lean over the side of the kitchen table to see what was underneath and "intercepting her thoughts." Then, amidst gazing a closer look at my purse, she asked me to put my *You Are My Sunshine* key chain away, as my late Grammie had "come along too!" Then, she swiftly blurted out how I was allergic to red dye, needed to drink more water and should always watch my diet since I have a tendency to welcome sweets. For the next several minutes, she would then have me silently sketch some drawings, now allowing her to "pinpoint the exact ages" where my emotional blocks were hindering most. Remarkably, she would illuminate how all the awesome revelations within this book were helping me to incredibly "rise" as well to a more appropriate age. At this point, with all this insight understood, I was more-than-ready to explore the uncomfortable issues that were seemingly stuck in my way. Now, she would begin to throw several once-familiar words out to me while I placed them along a timeline. Meanwhile here, my artwork would reveal a bag of heart-shaped buttons, a large black-and-white checkerboard, some carnival tickets, a black-beaded purse and my special Cinderella watch that had eluded my search for so long. It would also include a man in uniform, a heart-shaped tattoo, a childhood friend named Wendy, and lastly, a glistening array of red roses under a larger-than-life rainbow with a pot of gold at the end. Yet, now as push came to shove, I couldn't help but wonder; "What could all of these mystery *Life Is How YOU Look At It* tidbits possibly mean to me?"

As my past further unfolded, Minnie would next respond how I had at the age of six "scored an all around 'A' in Art Class, by making a beautiful paper maché puppet"—dressed in red checks with lace accents, amidst some heart-shaped buttons that I'd lovingly placed on the pockets. Around this same time she'd also envision me "sitting somewhere on the sidewalk with my head held in my hands." During that very summer, I had taken all my penny carnival tickets and entered them to win a tiny Beagle puppy. Then, once I'd actually won her, was so proud to return home. But, who would have thought that my sweet, little "Heidi" would only survive two more days leaving my hopes for the both of us (as I was harshly told to "get over it!") sadly dried up. Now, for the next jarred memory, Minnie would ask me who "Wendy" was. Here, I would reply how she was "a special friend since about fifth grade" who'd suddenly move away. Now, she would inquire as to what exciting-to-me occasion I had borrowed a black beaded purse. Seconds later, as the light bulb went on, I would recall the night of my Senior Class Banquet where I'd worn a pretty black-beaded and fringed jumpsuit with hat and purse to match. Moreover, my childhood friend Diane would then meet up with me in the bathroom, as arriving with different crowds. Next, she would produce a handful of rainbow-colored "secrets" that surely her unsuspecting parents had no clue about. Here too, I would tearfully gush to Minnie how awful I'd always felt because if I had only betrayed Diane's promised trust that night, she might still be here today. Now, as her voice would grow octaves softer, she would tenderly grasp my hand. Then, to lastly close out our session, she would also tell me how those purple Rosary Beads I kept stumbling upon resembled the same ones that were always draped across the mirror, in late Diane's once-teenage room! And, since never truly getting to say goodbye, they continued to trigger real hurt. Moreover, as exhausted as my brain now felt, I made another in-two-weeks appointment to merge with some more of my past.

Yet, my next encounter with Minnie would be even more enlightening than the first! After all, we next touched base on how at about the age of ten, I was sexually molested by someone I had trusted; leaving me alone with many AWFUL secrets no little girl should have to keep. Though, now was also the perfect time to take back my strength and spirit, as her solid grip held on ever-so-tightly, while we revisited that sordid room. Likewise, as she began to "get real" about these fearful surroundings, I got a better understanding of "all the shadows" I'd certainly felt as of late. You see, on the walls were nothing but a large black-and-white checkerboard made out of fur, that when combined with his many blinking strobe lights, had kept me as blind as Helen Keller! Next, she would also comment on the ever-nauseating mix of stale coffee, beer and cigarettes so encircling the room, and how together we'd be releasing their stronghold on my now, much-healthier senses. Likewise, "that heart-shaped tattoo" I'd once focused on to escape this ugly act, would now be left behind per Minnie—amidst my genuinely "re-born eyes" as an adult. Remarkably too, she'd take me next upon a "refreshing cleansing journey" that was comfortably visualized as though occurring "from behind the rushing waters" of Niagara Falls' natural bliss, so these once very-haunting revelations could now begin to rest in peace.

"When you ask for help from God and the angels, whatever the problem, their divine remedies usually lead to inner changes. As your life heals, it becomes increasingly difficult to tolerate situations, relationships, foods and locations that are no longer healthy for you . . . . You may start to question every part of your life: your marriage, career path, and home life. Your inner satisfaction seems to hinge on making healthy inner and outer changes."

~ Doreen Virtue, Ph.D

From "Rindercella" to Reality—and the Rainbows in Between!

After finishing up with Minnie, I was left in quite a lurch, as no longer "spiritually sandwiched" between my wounds and a New World. Next, I rediscovered how "We always fear the most during times of true transition—as our feet are never anchored upon any solid ground." Though gratefully too, the closer I got to enlightenment, the closer I got to God! Then, to my surprise, I began to "outgrow everything" that did not have my best interests at heart. Therefore, my life became more about really living authentically than any adrenaline rush! Gone too, were the days of compulsive shopping and binge eating to cope, amidst dead-end relationships filled with only sadness and strife. Incredibly also, the less frazzled my world would become, the more I could sense what to write! Besides, after Minnie's shocking breakthrough into the blocks of my childhood past, this once "black-sheep Cinderella" would never be the same.

It was a cloudy Saturday and only two days after that mind-blowing session, when I had just dropped my teenager off to a friend's house for the day. Suddenly, I had an overwhelming urge to pull off into a parking lot where millions of tears met up with me next. In the meantime, my flaming outbursts false insecurities and female-related illnesses all made sense at the flip of a switch! So, at this illuminating moment, I asked aloud to God: "Where shall I seek more of Your Wisdom out next?" And, after several cleansing breaths, my spiritual answer arrived. I'd now "be guided" to a nearby shopping mall to enter a reader's clearinghouse in search of my next clue. Yet, once parked in the area, a truly positive thought stopped me short in my tracks! From the front seat here, I took the time to absorb just how far I had actually traveled—amidst that previously written (almost five years ago) "The Poem That Wouldn't Leave Me Alone." To my further comfort, that "familiar feeling of warmth" overtook me when I saw how all these healing avenues I'd awakened weren't half as bad as running scared! Next, as my mind began to focus upon that poem's so-sacred preface, I saw the "tapestry-threaded meaning" behind two of its three signs! After all, the white dove pair I had originally envisioned unexpectedly appeared in "The Magic of My Michael's" miraculously just in time to teach me again to trust. Moreover, that single "flickering red candle" would manifest itself in Misfit's awesome pages, as the perfect little precursor to show me how love is "ultimately patient" as well. Meanwhile, in reviewing my Life Lessons amongst this enlightening adventure, the only thing now missing was the mystical explanation for that perfectly-colored rainbow with the pot of gold at the end. Therefore, seconds later I would find "the forever Nancy Drew in me" propped upon my knees in the carpeted bookstore in search of my next puzzle piece. When easily within minutes, my needle-in-a-haystack mission spoke loudly of success! See, I'd already known to begin my quest in the "Self Improvement" section, but was truly unprepared for what would illuminate me next. Here, as I courageously dug through the names of these semi-dusty books, one soothing-to-me cover, seriously caught my eye. While all decked out in shades of resounding color, it was its meaningful title which had my spirit solidly sold! Now, as I glanced down upon *Reach for the Rainbow,* I found it to be both a Godsend and a guidebook for all of us "Sexual Abuse Survivors" out there who, only years later, saw the light. And, even as my hands did shake as I post-traumatically paid for my purchase, I'd come too far to abandon ship: since I knew full well from my trusty purple-covered Bible's teachings how only the truth would set me free!

And, what a revealing life lesson it was in the words of Lynne D. Finney! Foremost, I would begin to learn "all about flashbacks" and how the more I talked them over with those I could trust, the quicker they'd surely fade. This sudden insight also showed me loud and clear why I'd been so scared to complete my calling, settling instead for several months of "created busyness" and being surrounded by some incredibly mean people; who would somehow gratefully become my catalysts to finally pushing me past the pain. Though, luckily as well, to shed further light upon the subject this lived-to-tell surviving expert would also wondrously write:

> "As adults, the fear we felt as children is triggered when we begin to recover repressed memories, just as other feelings we had during our abuse, such as anger and depression, are aroused. The child in us is terrified that if the memories come out and old feelings are experienced, we will go insane. Even though as adults we may want to recover our memories so we can heal as quickly as possible, part of us fights to keep them hidden."

Yet, once reading this "proof in the pudding," my pride went out with the wind! After all, this *Life Is How YOU Look At It* author would find increased faith in a fresh start! I would even be walking by the television to catch some still unknown-to-me speaker, positively explaining how, "Many wounded females who were sexually abused as children have a tendency to slip into a fairytale-like existence during those times as an adult when their worlds appear too stressed." Amazingly too, from my faithful doll Susie to colorful Cinderella collection, this timely puzzle piece would make real sense—as I'd come too far now amidst this calling not to finish out my dream. Finally, though it may have taken me over two years to digest all the *Reach for the Rainbow* facts, between fearfully ditching that book in a drawer, I too emerged a real "angel with a halo" once exposing the heartbreak of my own reality to help others reach new heights!

> "Accepting the fact that we were alone and that
> we survived—and *can* survive—is the last step in
> the healing process. And accepting the fact that
> we now live in a different world is the beginning
> of a new life.". . .
> "You can blame your abusers for the rest of your
> life, or you can get on with your life secure in the
> knowledge that *living well is the best revenge.*"
> ~ Lynne D. Finney

"What Are You Willing to Give Up to Achieve Your Dream?"

It was a drizzly January night. The kind where it felt best "just to stretch out on the couch" and catch up on some reading. Yet my relaxation would be short-lived as fifteen-year-old Bethany would soon return home with a dilemma after just having dinner out with her dad. Here, like every other "clueless parent," I was told how she needed a certain book from the bookstore by tomorrow for a class. With less than an hour till closing, I traded in my soft pajamas for a wrinkled sweat suit, and we headed out into the rain. On the way, I also shared with my daughter how truly irritated I was to be doing this errand so last minute. Yet once inside the bookstore, it would become very clear to me that Bethany was not the only one who was meant to be browsing so late. While she and some staff searched for that much-required reading, I found myself wandering amidst the "Self Improvement" aisle. Where at first, nothing seemed to catch my eye as I now stood face to face with many an author's front cover. Then on a whim, I whisked one book off to the left, only to discover Lucinda Bassett's latest work. Only this time, her subject was not about reducing the grips of panic and powerlessness, but living out an awesome "Life Without Limits." As I flipped through a few more pages, my lucid mind filled with a question that has surely changed my life, "What are you willing to give up to achieve your dream?" And here, like spilled milk to a paper towel, I was so thirsty for what I absorbed! Besides (like Lucinda), could it possibly be that this small town girl, now approaching her forties, still had some treasured dreams of her own to see through?

Once home with my new purchase, I continued to pour through the pages, when the subjects of "sacrifice and sabotage" truly stopped me in my tracks. Somehow, in less than three years, I'd faced my share of struggles, trading the woman I was striving to be just to tread water and keep us afloat. And, if the legal system wasn't enough aggravation, between delinquent child support hearings and drawn-out custody battles, seeing my niece Gina evolve into a taunted "special needs" student was almost more than my heart could take. As time revealed slowly, her misdiagnosed Autism worsened, Tourette's syndrome stood out, and her many seizures would set her apart from the "cool kids" attending their middle school. Sadly, in this nightmare's heyday, I couldn't allow my sister, Becky, to seek out these answers alone. Yet, even through all of this exhausting-at-times upheaval, a unique Gina would still remind us of her reasons on this Earth. When she was not actively seizing, she was an expert on the Titanic, and once even stayed "plugged in" enough to make the Honor Roll! Meanwhile, what an ugly drain her mounting bills had become on all our bank accounts as "the system" seemingly moved in reverse to get many medical or respite needs met. So, with fingers crossed, I would "summon more angels," and after almost five uphill years, the answers we'd been seeking slowly began to take shape. In retrospect too, I *Life Is How YOU Look at It* learned that family supports family, even at times when our own worked-for-goals were finally within reach.

Though, in the aftermath of this journey I awoke one morning with a feeling of outgrowing it all. But, like an ostrich whose head was once stuck in the sand, I emerged ready to figure out where I was. Then, before long while meditating the familiar words "What are you willing to give up to achieve your dream?" became not only a helpful mantra, but also a healthy mindset. And, as my flair again for writing began to freely color my world, I found myself faced with a million more choices. Meanwhile, in my heart's flurry to help out my niece amidst haggling in court, I'd ignored many red flags of my own. From my home to my workplace to an ongoing "kid in the middle relationship" filled with more resistance than respect—I knew I had to revamp my life, as our issues only get uglier until we readily address them. See, in regards to my stressful E.R. job, due to some "crass consultant's imposed changes" a part of me felt (until the day he was sent packing) like I'd truly sold out my soul. Here too, some of my favorite doctors would begin to leave or unfortunately were fired, while I was trying hard to convince myself that I could hold out on my fading desires until my own gifted Beth finished up high school. Then, on top of all this upheaval, I'd lost three very special people in only four short years, who'd also made me solidly promise as we still "spiritually connected," to forge through my real fear (without floaties!) of the unknown, and get this work put into print. More important, I knew it was hurting my self esteem more to dodge all the barbs that I was taking, then it was to design the strategy to put this sabotage to rest. Moreover, amid this startling realization, my thoughts again turned inward to revive those so-sweet tactics that had once really made me shine! In a heartbeat here, I joined a Wellness Group, went for weekly massage and found a church I felt at home at. I even uncovered Lucinda Bassett's once-so-inspiring tape program stuffed in a box underneath my bed! With each new day, I began to release the urge to always be there for others, in an all-out effort to let go of what wasn't working in my own life.

Miraculously too, "by simply saying no, standing still and scheduling my work around the people and places I adored," my exhausting load began to lift and energy abounded again. Then, amidst raw journal work, exercise came as a comfort, devotions gave me strength and I began to reconnect with all The Miracle Workers who'd made a difference in my rebirth. Though, carrying all this chaos had certainly left some craters for me to confront. Here also, like someone who'd just survived a tsunami, I arose ready to explore my own truths. First off, I knew most people in my life would only call while in the heat of some "feigned financial crisis," as only faking to be broke amongst airing out their guilt of having fun with everyone else. Second, while at my main job and being scolded regularly "not to talk too much with anyone" and all notified repeatedly how "you've each made another error," that once-so-sparkling environment seemed to have now settled, sadly for status quo. Finally, on the home front being "engaged to emptiness" hadn't fared well for me either, as I now felt strongly in my awakening how our "couple-hood" should come close to first. At the same time, I knew I was not only determined to finish these memoirs, but had also been distracted by a force bigger than myself! Therefore, I was not only quite miffed, but had also child-like fallen into feeling far more poor than positive by again "carrying other's baggage" that did not belong to me. Likewise, I couldn't help but wonder where the lady in me had gone, who'd learned to drive in a Chrysler Convertible, saw shapes amongst the clouds, and always planned on living somewhere, warm with sand to boot. Yet, while knowing God's always-with-me nudges would naturally get me through, there's a very special blessing in hitting rock bottom since there's nowhere to go but up.

What Are You "Willing to Give Up to Achieve Your Dream?"—Part II

To my further credit, I began to review the feedback I'd encountered, keeping me from pursuing this book. Though, overall the real fact remained, that I'd allowed myself to play it safe! Here too, starting with my family, I could painfully bring forth a conversation with my mom. Upon showing her a stack of my miracle-filled stories, she mundanely remarked something to the effect of, "Your writings are just like the hats I make Nan, nice enough to make others smile, but not enough to have you succeed." I could also remember an Easter Day dinner served at another member's household where I put my precious entries out for all present to enjoy. And, while no one even bothered to read them, my sister's reaction surprised me the most! It was later as I would share how I would hope to be on "Oprah," and while many of our friends would call to say that they'd seen me—she may someday be very sorry she never cared what made me tick. Furthermore, I couldn't help but feel that if I had gone to Grad school or was studying to be a doctor, I would be aided by those closest in a totally different light. Yet, *The Poem That Wouldn't Leave Me Alone* has held the key to my real calling, giving this petite, single mom working two jobs the power to succeed! Next, even as I found out that Oprah wanted to cancel her talk show, I planned to find another media outlet to spark the souls of others in need. Insightfully too, while the life-altering effects of my spiritual legacy may be limitless, I've been increasingly shown every day in the E.R. that my life span isn't the same. Then suddenly, like an "earthquake minus aftershocks," it all made sense to me! While mindfully trying to migrate back to "the bright side," sometimes reality overwhelms us with major bursts of rejection in order to take more risks! Besides, I would be much better able to provide for my loved ones by funneling my intuitive talents into an arena that I loved. Incredibly too, when my internal dialogue went from always "ask me" to assertive, then positive affirmations were planted like seeds within my spirit. Meanwhile, the "enlightened survivor" I am, also knew, this Life Lesson was more about enjoying the petals of the present by truly learning from past mistakes. So, with this insightful process blooming, I forged through the secretive wear-and-tear of "what Alcoholism causes a family," forgave all those I HAD enabled, and began to take the baby steps to make my goals my own. Next, I booked flights to see my girlfriends, bought some beautiful office accents and found myself feeling pretty in things I wasn't allowed to wear in years. Above all, I began to "get real" with reinventing my relationships—finding my fiancé also receptive to new boundaries for both our kids. At the same time, Oprah excitedly extended her talk show and continued to comment on her treasured book club, just like I'd envisioned that Easter. I even caught one special segment on the subject of "Divine Angels" and living out those lifelong dreams we've surely left on hold. And, it was here that I found myself totally brought to tears by the generosity of one pro football player. In honor of his late mother (a single mom sheriff who was shot in the line of duty, and left behind several young children to raise), this been-there-done-that hero surprises yearly, one deserving family with the means and the miracle of a home to call their own. Here also, Oprah would chime in about the forever-conflict of the single parent struggle, allowing more of my tears to flow. After all, we are the last to call in sick in case our children need us, do a lot that goes unnoticed and somehow in all the busyness find our yearnings coming last. Though if truth be told, while at first greatly uprooted by this "Single Mom slam," I feel so grateful to have cultivated my gifts amidst two almost-grown daughters and a created family of heaven-sent angels who continue to follow their hearts. Even my busiest workplace has improved greatly with increased two-way communication, amid a created Employee Recognition Program and ongoing renovations; becoming one of the top 100 places to work!

Furthermore, I've been shown the value of "punching in" as a productive partner, parent and poodle owner as sometimes life's presumed permanents are the ones we give the least. Wondrously too, I know a "Life Without Limits" doesn't happen without the likes of hope and faith. Though in closing, there are some things I truly do know for sure. First, I will only stay someplace where my input can matter, have plans to publish and publically speak and will never allow my lack of financial footing or forever "proving myself to painful people" to limit my agenda ever again. Also, I will be donating some of the proceeds from these precious works to Habitat for Humanity, allowing others to prosper primarily amongst real dignity and restored peace. Finally, while the time has come to find that convertible, finish this book before my twenty-fifth reunion and frolic in the sacred sun, I can't help but feel abundantly blessed. As over time, I have spiritually learned that outgrowing it all is not the end of the world, but the start of something big! Awesomely too, as my once blocked intuition screams "Go NOW for it girl!" my next mantra that hangs by my Wellness Class reads, because: "God Will Always Provide."

*** The above passage was completed a little over three years ago, and instead of manifesting my dream as hoped, I seemingly got derailed again by tons of negative stuff. Sadly too (I thought then), throughout this time of having almost "everything I considered a comfort, collapse" . . . (Pooh-Bear died, my girls got married or left for college, Beth's child support was court-ordered cut early, my car met the junkyard and I got ripped off remodeling my mobile home), I thought life surely couldn't get any worse than this! Though, I was truly unprepared for what would woefully occur next. One afternoon while racing home to check for mail at my earlier-moved-out-of mobile home, I'd be rounding the corner only to see several workers in the midst of bulldozing Poppy's so-memory-filled house into sheer rubble at the drop of a hat. Lastly, as I in-my-heart know how the "timing of this book's birth" is truly in God's hands, I was totally caught off guard by my fiancé's so loudly expressed anger over not wanting to help me to foremost lighten my load and that maybe we should take separate paths. After all, I knew our once church-going bond had more recently been at a crossroads, with one of me "being only able to write while swaddled amidst the Lord's warmth," while he continued only to slam on the brakes. So, as I sit here proof reading and still inspired with nothing left to lose, we'll see if when all is soon-to-be-done if "Good things come to those who wait" and God's Love will always provide.

With special thanks to Lucinda Bassett's *Midwest Center for Stress and Anxiety* and *Attacking Anxiety & Depression* home-study program for truly teaching me, though there's never a "right time" to tackle our fears; we rise and resonate more towards our true self each and every time that we take a risk.

> "I deserve to be happy, to feel content. I have
> the right to go after the things I want in life and I
> will achieve them."
> ~ Lucinda Bassett

The Midwest Center for Stress & Anxiety and the "*Attacking Anxiety & Depression*" program used by permission.

Reaching for Rainbows

If we don't ever take chances,
    we won't reach the rainbows.
If we don't ever search,
    we'll never be able to find.
If we don't attempt to get over
    our doubts and fears,
    we'll never discover how wonderful
    it is to live without them.
If we don't go beyond difficulty,
    we won't grow any stronger.
If we don't keep our dreams alive,
    we won't have our dreams any longer.

But . . .
if we can take a chance now and then,
seek and search, discover and dream,
grow and go through each day
with the knowledge that
we can only take as much as we give,
and we can only get as much out of life
    as we allow ourselves to live . . .

Then . . .
we can be truly happy.
We can realize a dream or two along the way,
and we can make a habit of
    reaching out for rainbows
        and coloring our lives
            with wonderful days.

~ Collin Mc Carty

"For where your treasure is, there your heart will be also.

Mathew 6:21

"NKJV ™"

My Life Is
How You Look At It Ending—
"When It All Suddenly
Made Sense"

One evening, I was taking an "Alpha Class" at a local Catholic Church as Luke had recently informed me during a much-needed massage, how this series may do my heart good. Meanwhile, each weekly session would begin by having our whole group meet for potluck. Then, we'd head off into the chapel for some special songs and a video tape. On this particular night, it had been really tough to get here as even from that hectic morning things had all gone wrong! Though once finally seated upon the shiny pew, I watched "all about those times when life seems so all uphill." Here too, an English-accented Nicky Gumbel would make my education easy, as he would next explain to his audience how "the closer we get to doing God's work" the more our goals may greatly derail. Naturally, I would be no exception as I'd just had another car accident, kept running into my "real father" (who would mostly look the other way), and had my single mom hands full at home with costly repairs and chronic health issues. At the same time, I promised God again that if He would just keep my gift of writing alive, I would not let Him down! Next, I began to "pick my battles" as needing to store some major energy to type amidst the pain I felt each day. But, for all those times I could not manage, I'd take it easy on myself. Besides, I knew the sooner I would finish my manuscript, the sooner I could be who I was. And, on that very evening as Nicky's lecture continued onward, I learned something so amazing that I almost fell on the floor. To my longing ears, he next made mention something about how "The only Father we'll ever need is that of the Lord's love," as God only lends us our "Earthly fathers" until He takes us eternally home. Wow! How much easier this made it to release my ongoing hurt, and choose the happiness of Inner Peace. Yet, the more I got a taste of Peace, the more I wanted it in ALL of my life. Then, I started to clean out my clutter at home from tarot cards to tucked-away stuff, and began to "do something special for another's deserving spirit each day" and tell no one else about it. When above all, my heaped-on housework would take a sudden back seat, to hearing what God needed me to write.

Meanwhile, the more I grew into myself as a beacon, the more others gave me a hard time! You see, I was seriously done with their drama, and the gossip had surely grown old. I would even be told very sternly sometimes how I "couldn't share pieces of my journey with some people, as my memoirs made others feel weird." Though for as much as I tried to stay quiet, the Holy Spirit continued to push! That's when Joyce Meyer's book *Life Without Strife* appeared and put these "seemingly put-down people" right into perspective as in one well-written paragraph she wrote:

> "Insecure people carry a root of rejection. They need a lot of outward assurance that they are accepted. They lack feelings of worth and value from within, so they crave it from outside sources. They need people to affirm their acceptance by their actions and words. The enemy uses people with emotional wounds and scars to stir up trouble. Of course, they don't intend to cause trouble, they only want someone to make them feel good about themselves."
>
> ~ Joyce Meyer

Now naturally, once blessed with this understanding, I could never go back where I was! Then, I also encountered here as well, a tidbit about "Mary of Guadalupe"—where a poor Indian man named Juan Diego was hand-picked to inform others of God's so blessed teachings. However, he'd been judged "too basic" by all his skeptics to ever seriously believe. Then, a few days later in 1531, upon being prodded to return to that same town, Juan now did as he was told. Though more than anything, he really dreaded taking this trip since that group of non-believers had also asked the Lord for "a special sign" to prove that his gift was real. Yet blissfully now, while on foot again, he couldn't believe his eyes! Jutting right out from the middle of this recently traveled mountain was a spectacular red rosebush, sent to set the town's people totally straight! Moreover, I saw while studying all about miracles, how "God loves to use the 'seemingly ordinary' (like me), to spread His Extraordinary Word!" Sweetly, for all the times I'd shy away from that which is my chosen purpose, He would send me spiritual signs as well to keep my agenda on course. Then, my Poppy would pick up right where the Lord left off as his "reincarnated red rose bush" continues to bloom at unexplained intervals too. For example, on Valentine's Day 2003, with eight inches of snow on the ground, amidst all those years when I was submerged in the custody/support courts—and even as my sixteen-year-old abruptly left home for all she thought that the world had to offer. Meanwhile, as God's persistence

continued to be my chief source of comfort, I made a pact
to both of us to get these enlightening pages completed by
September 30, 2006. Meanwhile, I even skipped a local,
summer Mark Wills concert (my favorite Country singer!)
and my twenty-fifth class reunion to keep this goal in check.
And, while forever being a single mom who really needed
to work, I took my downtime seriously and only "came up
for air" at intervals, for those considered my nearest and
dearest. Here, I gratefully found also, that for all those
times I would need to revisit an ugly issue to access the
Life Lesson, God's supportive words and wondrous Biblical
wisdom continually gave me strength. Remarkable too, even
at these confusing crossroads, I could always hear Him say,
"Keep plugging along, Missy, and set your fears aside—as it
will all make sense in the end." To which I would regularly
question "End, Lord? What end? What could my looming
Life Is How YOU Look at It ending have possibly left to
reveal?"

My Life Is How You Look At It Ending
Part II—When It All Fell Into Place

Two months ago, I was going over in my mind how
much I had grown from this book writing experience and
that original outpouring of "The Poem That Wouldn't Leave

Me Alone." At the same time, I had just finished reading *Life Without Strife*, and was busy putting Joyce Meyer's principles into place—from my reactions to my relationships, amidst beginning to ever consciously clean up my own act. Then, I was once again "drawn" to dabble in the pages of my above mentioned wondrous work, including all the mentors, Misfits and milestones. When suddenly, this very version made for a true miracle on paper, once deleting all the pain and defining all the positives!

The Poem That Wouldn't Leave Me Alone (revised)

I realized lately deep inside
That "things" felt incorrect.
What was it I was running from?
Or trying to forget?
I closed my eyes, went back in time
And saw the presence of two white doves.
Who gently sailed above my head
As I searched for my "Lost Loves."
First off, I was six again
And caught up with Diane,

Why she had died at twenty-one
Was so hard to understand.
She met me at our picnic spot
Our favorite sandwiches for two,
With Nestlé QUIK milk moustaches—
We talked a streak of blue!
She told me that living through all this,
Made me who I was today.
A compassionate, yet confident woman,
With a "gift for what to say."
Next stop was to my late Grammie's house
For Iced Oatmeal Cookies and some tea.
Where I told her how my love of both,
Keeps warm memories alive for me.
And how my warmest thoughts of her
Are carefree, warm and fun-
As I'll always remember that silk dress she made,
Bright and yellow like the sun!
As I joyfully kissed her soft cheeks goodbye
And turned away to leave,
I realized that my love of silk, lipstick and lotions
Were her legacies to me.
I thanked her for my sense of humor,
That at times is warm and witty.
While forever drilling through my head

Even in braces, I was PRETTY!

With that I climbed upon my doves

To meet up with "Lost Love Three"

As I rounded a cloud and looked around,

My father was waving to me!

Next, I gave him back his "poiple" juice,

Known as my favorite color,

Left him a box of English Leather

And went on to meet my mother!

She was window shopping at the mall

Like we always loved to do,

Teaching me how great it feels

To dress in something new.

She also sparked my love of surprises

With even presents on Groundhog's Day,

And showed me life is far too short

Not to reach for stars along the way.

Mom's even encouraged my creativity

To craft, to paint, to think . . .

So when she pops into my mind,

I always think of pink!

Remembering the time we prom-gown shopped,

At the fancy bridal stores were satin and lace,

Though, these expensive dresses did "nothing for me"

Destined to find it at my favorite place!

Here, the powder blue ruffled dress caught my eye

From the display window at my cherished mall,

Perfectly slipped from the mannequin, right onto me . . .

Like Cinderella on the way to The Ball!

The afternoon sun was now high in the sky,

As I bypassed more memories of gloom.

Then I spotted my Poppy outside in his yard,

Tending sweet lilacs, forever-in-bloom,

He's got a wonderful green thumb for caring,

For all the "transplanted children" he'd grown.

"Cause even if you weren't related to him,

You were nurtured like "one-of-his-own!"

He always finds just what to say

In a way I could never replace,

And knows my love of his fragrant, red roses,

Puts a smile on "his Missy's" face!

What pleasure there was as I took charge of my life

And gave this "Damsel in Distress" some new hope.

Now filling me up, with a soothing inner peace,

Instead of panic attacks and shopping to cope.

See, it takes more than just courage to delve into your past,

And face it layer by layer . . .

As "real healing" begins when the dark turns to light,

With the power of truth, love and prayer!

Then, I thought about those, who've helped guide me.

To make up the wonder of who I am now.

Yet, learning to free my own guilt and mistakes,

Has so enriched my existence, somehow!

And, from all of those people I have loved and lost,

I've associated each of them with a color.

While combining my strengths into the babe I've become,

Revealed a rainbow unlike any other!

Though, as the orange sun was setting, I realized

That my rainbow was incomplete.

I want to share my heart as well

"Based on trust" for my daughters to see.

It's time for me to love again,

To meet my inspiration, my best friend.

For my rainbow won't be finished,

'Til that pot of gold is at the end!

Lately I've felt him coming,

We were meant to be together.

I'll stand still and let him come to me,

Experiencing a miracle-filled forever!

See, there's truth in the fact we've lived parallel paths,

Littered with heartbreak, bad memories and pain.

Allowing us both to believe, that the strength of our love,

Promises NEVER to go there again . . . .

(*Note—About the same time, I'd be aimlessly shopping one day, and came across a really awesome vase in a variety store's reduced rack—that for only three dollars later, would further alter my ending's fate!)

> There are two choices to live out your days,
> Full of regret and afraid to take chances.
> Or risk yourself fully to find your authentic life
> Based on peace, fearlessness and slow dances!

Here also, I was prompted to review the sacred outline of "The Tapestry of Me" taken from this book's first few pages before continuing on with the above. When suddenly, it became very clear that all these *Life Is How YOU Look At It* "Saving Graces"—from sweet roses to recipes, amidst teachers and toilet paper—had each been spiritually manifested (even as my knees quivered!) to truly show me the light!

> So when each day dawns I will celebrate,
> The gifts of my hero, my angel my pal.
> Safely resting my head in the fortress of his arms,
> Proving God really answers "knee mail!"

He is the treasure I won't take for granted,

Knowing together, that we'll both grow old.

I am now prepared for Him to come,

I've seen the light, freed the doves . . .

FOUND THE GOLD!!

***Please turn here to photo on back cover!

Then, for all those times when I'd felt "fatherless, friendless or fruitless" in the framework of my polka-dot past, things as promised would fall into place. Likewise, while working one day at my hectic E.R. desk, a company-wide email called our "Thought for the Day" would land right in to my lap. Wondrously too, amidst providing the cherished "healing cement" for the enlightenment of my spirit, these precious words rang out like harp-filled music to my awestruck ears:

"We've been given only one piece of life's jigsaw
puzzle, and only God has the corners."

~ Author unknown

My "Life Is How You Look At It" Homestretch—From "Total Loser" to Truly Blessed!

> So Jesus said to them, "Because of your unbelief; for assuredly, I say to you, if you have faith as a mustard seed, you will say to this mountain, 'Move from here to there,' and it will move; and nothing will be impossible for you.
>
> Matthew 17:20
> "NKJV ™"

The eight months prior to originally submitting this manuscript were the hardest (I thought) of my life! As it seems, the more I trekked on towards the homestretch, the more my trials heated up. This was especially true on the home front, where I was repeatedly treated shamefully about my many single-mom bills and meager balance left in the bank. Though here also, there was something to cherish! After found to be "still standing once surviving last year's awful tsunami" (where other's heavy life loads landed all over me like hot lava from a volcano), I still maintained current payments and a mid seven hundred credit score! Yet, the hardest thing between the numbers crunch and feeling "like nothing" in the eyes of my once-supportive fiancé, was sensing how I was finally pursuing my publishing goal with a partner who just wasn't proud. Likewise, this scenario had never become more apparent than at his birthday lunch two months before. After all, we had been through a lot these past few weeks. Here, I positively assured "Allen" how we'd even managed to "ace our smallest dog's latest illness with still enough money to pay our monthly bills." Next, I told him how these struggles were simply "a bunch of relationship tests we'd only survived with God's help" and by totally believing in His Blessings, the best was yet to come! Then, it was at this point that he would heart-wrenchingly lash out about how I couldn't even afford to help pay for a certain saw he'd set his sights on, as it really would have been the perfect present to his talented finish of remodeling our porch. And, before I could even begin to blitz back with, "Don't you think I'm aware that my mobile home isn't selling amidst our sorry economy, and my college honor student's car payment has somehow landed right back in my lap?" I was *Life Is How YOU Look At It* blindsided by the ugliest public outburst I'd ever endured in my life! Angrily, I would be told how "us ever getting married and having your bills paid off would be as much of a frickin' miracle as your book ever getting published!" Woefully next, while finding myself speechless in my most painful moment ever, I think the saddest part was realizing that we were spiritually now on separate pages (while the tender topic of one's "selective panic over parting with money" became more like his middle name.) Now, as my heart ripped to shreds, I'd honestly answer Allen with how "the toughest part of my sustaining all these struggles is that you still see me as a total loser." To which he abruptly fired back "You are a TOTAL LOSER!" and got up to settle our bill. Then, in the next few months we would be meeting with a Presbyterian pastor, where he'd explain to both of us not only our roles in God's eyes while becoming Bible-based partners, but that "if she has some bills, Sir, then you have bills too." He also would try to teach us the religious concept of "tithing" as the more we'd certainly give away to the church, the more we'd reap in return. Lastly, he would encourage us to not only "be accountable to God but also to each other" by always retreating inward, not running away whenever things got tough. So, needless to say, our potential wedding day came and went amidst an "if you can manage to x, y and z in my book," then we might get married some day by a Justice of the Peace. Above all, this unexpected "slam-dunk" after flunking Allen's own test of "for richer and for poorer" was now only half as hard as living sinfully with someone, yet feeling totally alone. Meanwhile, I silently mourned the loss of my best friend whose once so-steady support had been my soft place to fall. At this point too, it was abundantly clear (amidst no more of our once "what's mine is yours" merging mindsets) that he would be firmly hanging on to all his worldly goods, while I could financially hang by myself. But, in my heart I also knew how "anyone can get married," though the devoted couples have the tools in place to deal with life's woes when they hit. And, though we'd already conquered "For better and for worse" and "in sickness and in health" I thought with flying colors, the devil was working hard on forever keeping that "TOTAL LOSER thought" forefront in my mind. Besides, it would have been much easier to flog Allen for such heightened ugliness then to ever try to forgive. So, with baby steps, I started to attend my childhood church again where I'd always gone to Brownies. I hoped that God might still have some insights to aid me in "either living with, or leaving behind" a life based now only on lines in the sand. Here too, at every sermon given by Father Noah, I wished for some sacred tidbit to help my self-esteem recover, as when others keep on "totally ripping us apart" they are most unhappy with themselves.

Yet, foremost over that summer too, I would discover an awesomely written book entitled *Love & Respect* from the wisdom-filled encounters of Dr. Emerson Eggerichs. This was a right-what-I-needed awakening regarding what actions I, as "a wanna-be-successful-writer, yet continuously-in-conflict-woman-at-home," HAD done to help botch a once very beautiful relationship loaded with roses and respect. I would also rediscover a wonderfully written-from-years-ago e-mail from a spiritually in-tune-with-me Allen, that when he wrote of how "my unconditional love had healed all the holes in his heart," I could not help but cry. Here also, Joyce Meyer's *Enjoying Everyday Life* revelations would reappear each weeknight for fifteen minutes from the radio in my car. And, on one such July night, I knew she was speaking right to me! Moreover, she was telling her audience this evening something to the effect of: "If you are finding your life load totally exhausting, then simply live off God's vine for a year." She also went on to elaborate how "someone out there is so incredibly gifted" that even if she could crawl out from the radio she would encourage them to never give up. Furthermore, I was hard-and-fast approaching "Burn-out Boulevard" myself from this ongoing spiritual warfare and being "unequally yoked" at home. Meanwhile, over the months, I would delightfully learn as well, how during those times when others deem us most worthless is the time God wants us the most! Next, I'd also be tackling Joyce's mindful suggestions of "zipping my lip" while examining my OWN poor choices and began practicing being the first in line to forgive. Besides, what did I really have to lose by giving away my special possessions and going with God's guidance one hundred percent? Though, the hardest part in putting faith first is when He kept on telling me to do some things that didn't seem to make any sense!

"Character cannot be developed in ease and quiet. Only through experience of trial and suffering can the soul be strengthened, ambition inspired and success achieved."

~ Helen Keller

My "Life Is How You Look At *It* Homestretch"—Part II

From "Mumbo-Jumbo" to Making Sense

As previously mentioned, Father Noah's special sermons were giving me such hope! It was now late Fall 2010, with the chill of winter's approach in the air. On this specific Sunday, as our Reverend softly spoke to his hungry congregation, what he would enlighten all of us next with was just what I needed to know! Here, he would encourage each of us weekly worshippers to: "Whenever you hit the rough times, remember to ALWAYS focus on up." (Besides, Satan and "some lost folks" will surely lurk under the surface attempting to sabotage any goodwill mission; yet, by fixating our eyes on God's Love destroys any chances of that!) Though, as I began to firmly focus instead of foremost falter, the "hot seat" where I was sitting at home began to seriously heat up! See, there was an ongoing tug-o-war over my timely completion of housework versus manifesting "His work." So, I would get up in the overnights to allow more time to write. Besides, more than anything, Allen was peeved over my inability to have my writings flow on ANY other computer but his main one that was perfectly parked within the dining room with that great view of all his sports. Even though he had thoughtfully purchased separate laptops for our whole family as early birthday/Christmas gifts at the beginning of the year! And, while I didn't quite understand the rationale behind "only being able to type on his stuff" either, I certainly knew how much Satan loves to stir up loads of strife. Yet, God will also continue to place a couple in some very uncomfortable situations until they find the compromise "to finally get it right." So, needless to say, my partner worked on grumbling less often, my life's legacy was almost done! On the flip side, I kept on reading books like *Love & Respect* by Dr. Eggerichs, and was trying to be more honorable to Allen regardless of any ripples he'd cause. After all, he was a great single dad, a hard-working man and still such a laugh-loving softie to almost everyone else! Looking back too, it made me smile to remember how he was once so good to my daughters, as sadly anything awesome they did now was only crankily condemned. Therefore, could it be that he was not only frustrated over our lagging situation, but now lacking the sweet blessings of any spiritual input, leaving the "most romantic man I'd ever dated" totally overwhelmed?

Then, once I realized that I didn't have to be his human hacky-sack or Holy Spirit any longer, mother and the maid or the butler and the babysitter, I freed up way more time for God. Almost overnight too, I easily began to write again and appreciated Allen's strong points (instead of harboring on his "stuck points") truly so much more. Besides, even with his four-year fight with a real life-changing illness, he'd still managed to take us on two remarkable trips this year! One was an incredible journey to Washington DC in honor of my step-son's sixteenth birthday, where The White House was so much more beautiful when viewed with one's own eyes! The second was a scheduled trip to Vermont that was supposed to have been our honeymoon. How wonderful it was to hike in the woods, see all the leaves change, pick out Christmas presents for loved ones and get lost in the stores and shops. It was ever-so-relaxing just to lounge on our balcony, build warm wooden fires, and enjoy sweet and syrupy apple cinnamon pancakes each morning as we got up. Though, as it would sadly "resonate" also over-and-over in my mind that we were nowhere near getting married, I thought it still spoke volumes we'd somehow managed to both show up. Yet, here as well, I made a promise to myself. Where from the heart, I would be prayerfully asking God for more of His illuminating wisdom to aid me in finally facing "all those intuitive butterflies that kept gnawing at my insides" the minute we got home. Because I knew, although Allen and I seemed to love each other, some things just weren't adding up.

Once back in town, I began to meditate on what was causing our couple-hood to struggle the most. So here, it seems our biggest conflicting issue (that I now only as "a bird on the balcony" could see!) was less about being hard headed with each other, but more about letting God be the head of our roost. And, as I dug deeper into this train of thought, I realized that Allen had felt from a few years ago that I should've filed bankruptcy, and heard many times at nausea also "if only YOU had done 'a, b and c' we'd be in such a better place!" That's when I would answer back how God would tell me as I prayed that I "was not to file for bankruptcy, but to get some solid Christian-based financial guidance (thanks Dave Ramsey!), and begin to learn from past mistakes." He would also remain firm that a bankruptcy blemish would not allow us to move out as a family from a "way-more-crime-ridden-area" to a way more write-friendly place. Meanwhile, as I decided to solidly flow with this subject, I realized more things as well. As woefully, Allen would also tell me in a primarily disgruntled groan that "you should have just dumped off your mobile home years ago and then published your book as YOU'D planned." Yet, each and every time I brought these two things to the Lord, He would assure me to "wait patiently my child, and you will know when MY time is right." Besides, my mobile home was truly the only equity I owned. Therefore, it was so easy to see that the more I was meekly growing with God, the more we were growing apart! Next, my mind flashed back to those "pre-marital consults" we'd had with that pastor where he would (amidst discussing also, one's so fervent at-times anger) make a triangle shape with his hands. Shortly thereafter, he would explain that for any marriage to work our true priorities should be focused on God first, our sacred vows second, then having those family, work etc. pieces all falling underneath. And, while he continued on to educate those things considered front-and-center for half of us (like always being consumed about money, skipping church for the work team's baseball and acting better to everyone else), it became real crystal clear to me why our talk-time had crumbled and the tsunami's had set in! Moreover, when we were expected to be accountable to each other and wait humbly upon God's blessings, it was so much easier to bail out then to see what His strength had in store. After all, this new way of "Christian living" was also news to me. So, with this illuminating insight, I made an appointment to see Father Noah, because I had some unanswered questions that could surely use his expertise.

Upon arriving at our late October meeting, my cherished cleric was glad to see me. Within minutes, he was more than happy to filter my questions, so I was free to fire away. First, I explained that after leaving behind the comfort of my cocoon to become a new beacon/butterfly/book writer, although I was thankful God had chosen me, exactly where was He now? Especially since my world was hitting the skids? Besides, I had promised Him that if He should restore my gift of writing, I would do WHATEVER effort it took to faithfully get to the finish. But, where was His solid guidance, since my mobile home wasn't selling and I no longer fit my own life? And, what if I'd already cashed in on all His life-sustaining miracles when it came to helping me? Then, with a smile and a nod Father Noah would reply: "Continue to pray and practice patience my dear, read your Bible and live to learn. If you do, God can't help but reward you!" Here too, he would further enlighten me "how the conclusion piece of any book's makeup is always the hardest part to write." Then, I would also share next that Our Lord kept telling me since early August how I "was to stay humbled and humiliated in silence, continue to dwell in the hot seat (a.k.a. that dreaded home computer), and if this stress would get too much for me I should lose that last twenty pounds!" So, I would next comment to my special Reverend amidst rolling my eyes, "Isn't it wonderful that God still keeps a sense of humor when he sticks us doing something we hate?"

Now, he would inquire about how Allen was and how his health was holding up. To which I would answer back how he was seeing a new doctor and holding his own at stress-filled work. I also informed Father Noah that our Vermont trip went very nicely, though I myself was struggling with both "not having a solid commitment, and amidst my increasing loyalties to the Lord, always going alone to church." After all, who was I supposed to listen to—the one who easily used to invest in our love or the God that ULTIMATELY believed in my life? Finally, I would tell him how much I was truly dreading the approaching anniversary of our first date—as every holiday since the previous November was either so supremely sabotaged or super sparkle-free. (Besides, how many couples do you know whose car transmissions go on not only a Sunday evening but what was also Valentine's Day as well?) Lastly, I explained how the harrowing task of finding a publisher felt more like I was "actually climbing Mt. Everest" than even had half a clue. Now, as Father Noah began to chuckle, he would totally help my dilemma by truly reminding me of something that I *Life Is How YOU Look At It* already knew! If my heart remained open to answers, the answers would always arrive. In the meantime, he would state how I'd "need to walk GRATEFULLY in baby steps" toward the goal of getting published. Yes, the same baby steps it would take Allen to ever go back to church.

A word fitly spoken is like apples of gold In settings of silver.

Proverbs 25:11

"NKJV ™"

My "Life Is How You Look At It" Homestretch—Part III

From "Light bulb Moments" to Living The Dream

Your word is a lamp to my feet And a light to my path.

Psalm 119:105

"NKJV ™"

At our next church service, Father Noah would be bubbling over with more of his contagious charisma to help us foremost to cope. From his usual place behind the pulpit he would tell us all to "Instead of always trying to look before you leap, make a totally courageous effort and just Leap before you Look!" He would also assure us that God would be solidly behind us after the fact to see our life's journey bear sweet fruit. Then, about a week later too, he would call my cell phone saying how much he needed to see me. So, shortly thereafter I would "clueless worse than usual" arrive at the church to see what was in store for me next. And, as I found my Reverend comfortably seated in his several candle-burning office, I was in for the surprise of my life! Held in his hands was a mainly "for clergy brochure" he'd always gotten in the mail—yet this month's insightful edition was so much more than that!

You see, while also unknown to me, Father Noah had been busy saying some unanswered prayers of his own! Next, he explained how he'd known of a certain Christian-based publisher that several of his friends had used, but when it came time to truly enlightening me further, he just couldn't remember their name. That was, until this early November week when the newest edition arrived. Here, when my clergyman as usual opened this book to casually flip through the pages, that publishing company's colorful advertisement would be the one to greet him first. Needless to say, with this "truly in-God's-timing" information in hand, my "Leap before You Look" challenge had sweetly grown by leaps and bounds!

Enter November 14, 2010. And, while it was no surprise next that Allen would both not remember our anniversary again and easily forget (amidst discussing my upcoming weekly chauffeur list) that my birthday was just four days away! Though, even recently preoccupied by nursing back an injured shoulder and the soon-to-be start of hunting season, I was totally shocked as that intuitive "churning butterflies situation again reappeared" that I'd "crappily" encounter next. See, "if your mate starts acting squirrelly", dwells increasingly on all YOUR faults (in his eyes) and especially forgets those things important-to-you-as-a couple, yet needs to always pinpoint your evening schedule so his phone calls can come in, seems nine times out of ten, they're busy leading an alternate life. Yet, at this time too, I'd be wondrously reading Jill Kelly's *Without A Word* about the heart-wrenching "trials then transformations" the Lord's love had made in her whole family—especially amidst her husband, Jim, when his world came crashing down. And, like Jill, while I could really relate most to wanting to just ball up on the floor of my closet, God kept on telling me that "it wasn't time to confront this, and to remember to FOCUS only on up." After all, if I suddenly derailed while surely in the last leg of this gifted mission, I would not only miss my two rapidly approaching deadlines, but Satan would win as well. Positively too, I wanted more-than-anything to get this book off the ground around Mother's Day, as not only did raising my two daughters delightfully help this to happen, but wanted to also give them their copy on a day that means so much. Over time too, though I more than knew how I was responsible only for my own choices, it didn't make it any easier to know that others were emotionally getting Allen's "good side" that should've been saved for me. More important, why are so many people out there who "consider themselves 'T' for taken"—even enticingly along for the ride? Especially while they are so busy investing in each other, as their "supposed inconvenience" unknowingly (they think) sits home?

Though, remarkably next, I would speak to a woman at the publisher right before my birthday, who would also illuminate me that "the very time to pursue my writing venture couldn't be more perfect" as they were having a pre-Black Friday special that would save me thirty percent! And, with no other way to begin to afford this, I called the only credit card where I had any leftover credit to see if they might send me new card, as I hadn't touched theirs in years. To my surprise, the lady at the company would tell me something so truly amazing that even as I type this, I know, was more than a twist of fate! Here, she would next enlighten how this (not-requested-by-me) card was already mailed out incredibly two days earlier, as they were running a promotion through January that all purchases were interest free! So, while this action spoke loudly of such a "trustworthy God sticking His nose awesomely again in my business," I was also beyond thrilled to know that my most painful birthday ever week wouldn't be a total washout. Likewise, even my new girl, Beth, at work had remembered my special day with a beautiful 15 x 15 piece of artwork inscribed, "Home is where your story begins." Where blissfully too, while others seemingly could have cared less, these bestowed gifts were the best of my life.

At this juncture, Allen would regularly update our family about how he "couldn't wait for all his bills to be paid off by next summer and would be happy when he'd stashed several thousand in the bank." He was also looking forward to the time when I (with some of this book's proceeds) could buy him some prime hunting land and help to pay for a new house as well. And, each time I would answer him back that "I'd given my financial picture to God who'd put me on a five-year plan," dead silence, of course, would ensue. All this, as my youngest was struggling for basics in college, her part-time job prospects were primarily wilted and she was sacrificing without a car. Moreover, why did it always feel in our new lopsided attempt to communicate, like a "take-a-number on his side" and a two-way street on mine? And, while I so now enjoyed being a step mom, I saw how our most relentless issue wasn't "really all about finances," yet one of us facing his own "Mt. Everest fears" without The Faithful Trinity's base on which to fall back! Here too, while I wanted so much to throw Allen an anchoring life preserver, the Lord kept telling me he would have to learn this so-awakening life lesson of "being truly impossible to love both God's ways and one's assets at the same time" seriously on his own. Besides, for all those times that I too had fallen off the Lord's wagon, it felt so good as "His lost child" when I was always with open-arms welcomed back! Though, as no surprise next, a rash of things kept on breaking at home amidst needing rapid replacement, and our littlest puppy's vet bills again went right through the roof. Yet, with every household crisis we sustained, the simpler I'd become. So much so, that I was less concerned with any money I'd make, and more with getting, this divine work wondrously out to enrich others, once patiently put into print.

Miraculously too, the more I entrusted God to handle, the more gifts of extra hours, checks and bonuses at work continued to come in. After all, I wasn't "being lazy" by adjusting my life load, but letting the Lord increasingly vessel through me! Woefully too, while someone routinely talked in "I" statements (though I'd always remind him how "we were a WE"), I found myself feeling foremost like both God and I had assumed a place on his surely "everything-else-first priority list" on the soles of each of his shoes. Then unexpectedly, upon listening to some Christian-based show, I'd also found how "Men are not only to be the overseers of household finance", but are also slower to come to Christ due to some ongoing power struggle that their submission seems to provoke. But, more than anything in my studies, I saw that Jesus doesn't eternally linger over us but loves to be INVITED in. And, this usually doesn't happen for anyone until we make peace with our pre-God pasts.

Furthermore, I was truly hurting at home as there weren't any "compliments for centuries," amidst the daunting reality that no one's eyes were excited to SEE ME anymore or ever lit up when I walked in the room. I was also especially tired of grieving our faithful dog (for fifteen years) Pooh-Bear's death all alone. As somehow, it seemed that each and every time some memory would trigger my tears I'd inappropriately be snapped at, though, when others called with such heart-wrenching woes Allen compassionately became all ears. But, more than anything I knew, I didn't want to bear the emotional brunt anymore of all this uphill baggage where one of us was expected to be accountable, yet the one who was supposed to be cherishing my heart couldn't be an open book. Besides, I think one of our biggest challenges as a couple was exactly how much I'D CHANGED, while my editor Phyllis would explain how I could now very much relate to spiritual "God speak," sounding more like gibberish to somebody else. When suddenly here, an unexpected handful of Christian people appeared consciously encouraging me to just "Believe in all I could be!" Even Josephine would teach me next what it meant to be "anointed" and promised me explicitly that if I continued to give my all to this writing venture, then God would do the rest. Yet, who would believe this obvious (though off-the-wall at times) outpouring of unconditional love, unless they had truly lived it? Therefore, if the Lord could be this gracious, then I would need to be grace-filled too.

So, as Father Noah had suggested, I would keep on reading my Bible for more sacred passages to help this so-surreal experience sort of make some sense. Meanwhile, I (like many others) had heard the phrase, "For the love of money is the root of all kinds of evil." But, when put into full Biblical context, they'd left off the very best part! From 1 Timothy 6:9-11, I would learn how: "But those who desire to be rich fall into temptation and a snare, and into many foolish and harmful lusts which drown men in destruction and perdition. For the love of money is a root of all kinds of evil, for which some have strayed from the faith in their greediness, and pierced themselves through with many sorrows." Then, excitedly I read as well, "But you, O man of God, flee these things and pursue righteousness, godliness, faith, love, patience, gentleness." Likewise, in my own words I now saw clearly how the key to an abundant life is less about holding on tightly to all of our things, and more about loosely letting them go! Though, here too, I felt a real sense of sadness as one-half of us continued to "cast her cares upon the Lord" while the other (amidst his ongoing list of my unmet conditions) was so confusingly lost.

Incredibly, about the time of typing the above, I would catch another of Joyce Meyer's enlightening messages, though I "hadn't in my busyness" been tuning in for weeks. Here, she was foremost going on all about her husband Dave's "seeming inability to do things" whenever SHE saw fit. After all, he had a loud and sporty "mid-life crisis car" just sitting in their garage. And, more than hating to ride in it, Joyce hated making the payments on it more. At this point, her husband would humorously walk up on the stage, taking over the *Enjoying Everyday Life* microphone, to divulge the rest as he knew it should go. Then, while she would so laughably beg him not to do it, I couldn't wait to hear the last part! See, while Dave was one hundred percent fine with waiting upon God's sacred timing, his controlling wife couldn't stand to do the same! Therefore, as Joyce would now continue on with completing the story, even the car's costly engine would go when one of their sons needed to borrow the keys. Needless to say, this car that was driving her crazy wasn't going anywhere fast. Yet, in the end, this dreaded car wasn't left around by God because it was "her husband's fiasco," but used by Him to teach an unwilling Joyce to finally cast her cares. Next, while seemingly everyone was laughing so hard that tears ran down all our faces, I fully understood how "sometimes when we've been unfairly judged to be such TOTAL LOSERS" is spiritually when God shows us that the problem isn't always ours. Talk about bells and whistles! Wow, the mobile home wasn't selling, our money was tight and this book hadn't launched in "Allen's expected timeframe" because he wasn't willing to let God into both his heart and his home to optimally do any work. Besides, what a wonderful way to say goodbye to my "deemed uselessness" and free up more positive energy to get this final piece to flow. Incredibly too, any time it would seem that my writings would basically wither, I'd always then stumble right upon another of the Lord's enlightening Bible verses to blissfully water my works!

Meanwhile, amidst my mindful gravitation towards God's "My Way or the highway" daily dose of meditation, the more berating my partner would get with me, and the more determined I would become. Here too, I would get the ugly "sinus ache-all-over sickness" for about two months, while finding it almost impossible amongst my increased work schedule to even willfully wake up and write. Yet, at this time, God would humorously enlist the help of my precious puppy "Bandit," because "even if it was still really dark outside and almost a quarter-to-three, he'd pester me with his busy paws till I arose to take him pee!" Though, more than anything, I saw that when I promised the Lord I would do "WHATEVER effort it took if I too, like Laurel, should be borrowed as a beacon" I had my work cut out for me. (While suddenly, also experiencing at home that oh-so familiar-from-childhood sensation of "shriveling up inside amidst AWFUL 'gut rot' again, like I now lived with my first grade bully"—while God was so solidly, "Fear not I am with you" NOT letting me off the hook and saving my hardest Life Lesson for last!)

> I hate the double-minded, But I love Your law.
> You are my hiding place and my shield; I hope in Your word.
>
> Psalm 119:113-114
> "NKJV ™"

Bandit's puppy picture
2008
(Yes, that's his tail on his head!)

"The enemy wants you consumed with hopelessness and will tell you all sorts of things about yourself, your life, other people, and God if he thinks you will believe them and lose hope. But the devil is a liar; you must not believe anything he says.

Remember, God has thoughts and plans for your good, to give you hope for your future. If you will hold on to your hope and fight for it when the enemy tries to take it away, you will see amazing things take place in your life. Being hopeful helps you to press on instead of giving up."

~ Joyce Meyer

(From NEVER GIVE UP! by Joyce Meyer.
Copyright © 2008
by Joyce Meyer. By permission of Faith Words).

"Many persons have a wrong idea of what constitutes true happiness. It is not attained through self-gratification but through fidelity to a worthy purpose."

~ Helen Keller

My Life Is How You Look At It Homestretch Part IV—

From Born A Miracle to Best for Last

It was now almost the second week of December. Here, my red-checked manuscript had been returned from Phyllis, who was not only my Christian editor but had also from-the-heart waved her fee. Gratefully too, I'd be scheduling some nose surgery for early next year amidst these three goals to truly be able to breathe better, get this corrected-version punctually up and running and to recuperate in peace. At the same time, Allen seemed more financially seething, somehow needed his computer more and was also getting more frequently sick. As our household woes continued to escalate, the general feeling as I forever prayed felt more like the "Great Divide" then foremost Divine Guidance. After all, as Allen would talk at times of "us getting married down the road" and the special trips he wanted to take (once I'd

237

managed to scale Mt. Everest), the utmost of all realities was that his willful increase in "sidestepping-us activities" wasn't mirroring the same. In the meantime, while I was past the point of plunging headfirst into the homestretch, Father Noah would continue to brighten any of my life's bleakness with the thoughts that left his tongue. And, on this particular Sunday, he'd be discussing the roles of "a believer" meshed with a "non-believer," and that by living by example one may truly show the other the healing power of God's Holy Light. Here too, he would go on to say not to expect this effort to be easy, as many others who've bravely "withstood such brokenness" have stood very much alone. But, he would also make it clear that if within any marriage the non-believer chooses to leave this spiritual imbalance, one should as The Bible instructs, simply let them go. While I had no problem understanding this principle, I did not know if I wanted to take on this truly heavy (and non-married) load in the middle of finishing this up. Yet, when dealing with God on His terms, you don't always have a say! Then, at this very minute, my mind flashed back to attending that final "Alpha Class" with Allen many moons ago. Next, I remembered how awesome it felt to receive our "spiritual gifts," as this was such concrete confirmation that there really was a God! As remarkably within seconds, my mate was given the "gift of prophesy," while I now sacredly spoke in tongues. So, was it really any wonder that the devil wouldn't leave us alone?

Shortly thereafter, as Christmas approached, one of my friends found herself unexpectedly brought to tears. After all, it was supposed to have been a wonderful night for her and her significant other. Full of the traditional magic and music they always shared preparing their family for Christmas, amidst a stunning picturesque DVD and some cups of hot cocoa to boot. Yet, on this particular night, her lover seemed very distant. And, although planning to leave later for a short family obligation, he wrapped a few of her presents abruptly; yet couldn't keep his focus off the ticking clock. Then suddenly, instead of singing along to the carols, he went into "such a tizzy" over not being able to locate his phone. When minutes later, he slipped out the door to safely receive that call from his "work spouse," a word I had once read somewhere that still turns my stomach today. Here, as my sweet pal painfully sobbed into my ear, I was left only to pick up the pieces amidst truly wondering, "Why do people even bother to get married if they aren't willing to do all the work?" Meanwhile, my friend was far from alone in her struggle. Seems everywhere I looked this "sister on the side" or "work spouse thing" was truly on the rise. Yet here, I can only pray for all those "Emily's" and "Edwards" out there who are so busy leaving their "loved ones" at home, can find renewed faith amidst God's inspiration to salvage their own relationships instead of always robbing from somebody else.

Next, Allen would start to ruminate over "all we weren't affording for Christmas," and I would smile respectfully, knowing I had some surprises up my sleeve. After all, the puppies had purchased him a new digital camera and were sending him on a secret scavenger hunt complete with written clues! I also celebrated, here as well, how both my girls would be home too. Though, in the holiday hustle, my mate would seem more tired, wasn't watching his diet and kept coming home to dwell on all the work "we" needed to do. Then, just when I thought that our Christmas might be all out of miracles, he joined me back at late-night church.

The last week of December 2010 was crazy beyond belief! As the single mom working two jobs (amongst that really-striving and under deadline book writer I'm so aiming to be), I was very busy in E.R. all day and buried later in my retail store's rush. Here too, I would learn how my closest friend, Denise, had suffered a heart attack on Christmas and was now scheduled for some surgery on the very same day as mine. Therefore, I would be begging God also to please "not let me lose another girlfriend, especially before I'd published" as she'd always been such a believer in my spiritual "bumper car's" path! Though for Denise and I both, time was very much of the essence. After all, her insulin pump was now failing as well as her eyesight, due to her long-term bout with Juvenile Diabetes, and I needed to review my entire manuscript and type any necessary changes all within a post-op month. At the same time, God would reappear with His latest round of High Expectations. Next, He would share how He was truly proud of all my progress. Then, He asked me to still "submit to this work in silence around your painful once-believer." He also informed me that although my mobile home would be selling around spring, I was to "humbly let it go to the lady," even though it would feel like I "took a hit." Then, the Lord would tell me how all those vanilla cookies I was downing to cope each night, weren't doing a thing for shrinking my waist! Next, He would also make it clear that the reason He had chosen NOW to have me punctually complete this calling, was because whenever push came to shove previously amidst all the stress, I'd proven my will to persevere. Finally, I would tell Him how I was struggling most with "the very last part of this section," as I couldn't seem to locate the right author's excerpt to make heads or tails of His most recent (half-crazy!) requests. Meanwhile, the task of totally sitting that "hot seat" was forcing me to LOOK at my life! And, what better way to get all-aboard with God then to willfully release my mobile home (though really wanting to "beep-beep" back there like the Road Runner!) and should my life truly fall to pieces, have nowhere left to go? Then, right about here, I began to review my precious writings for any insights I might have missed. After the fact, I planned to pursue my New Year's resolution of forging a more peaceful coexistence, especially amongst those who've "hurtfully wronged me and those I've wrongly hurt." Meanwhile, amidst my free-flowing visions, I found myself once again awakened at all hours of the night.

Then, as I began re-reading all the intuitive stories I had *Life Is How YOU Look at It* written, though not in any specific order, they spoke volumes for all I'd learned. When I started off with my "sister and her family's very special story," I couldn't help but laugh again when my little niece, Gina, took the ugliest of brown crayons and let loose upon my cupboards! About this time too, Father Noah would have more wisdom for me to savor. See, one evening during our wintry evening Eucharist service, he would stop what he was reading and point over to the wall. Shortly thereafter, he would knowingly explain how "Any time we are feeling less-than-special, if we immerse ourselves in God's soothing light" it's like applying that perfect coat of paint over top that no longer lets our imperfections show.

A few nights later, I would also be revisiting my much-loved work entitled "The Magic of My Michael's." While more-than-knowing how the special men named "Michael" always have the most to teach me (amongst their real angelic tendency to appear right out of the blue), I was even more amazed at the sudden enlightenment my "cooing-dove soul sister's" section sweetly shed instead! See, it had already been revealed, amidst this passionate story's ending, how with only a "pinch of angel dust" to show for my efforts I'd be pursuing this last leg alone. But, to me, "all alone" was defined as one thing and to Almighty God surely another! So now, like always, I'd surrender my situation to His Sacred Hands to see what would happen next. Therefore, you can imagine my delight when a soft-spoken gentleman carrying a book in his hands appeared at my desk a few days later. While at first it seemed that "Lester" was only interested in getting some directions, then with a magnetic smile that moved mountains, he mirrored several of his thoughts out to me! Here too, he would comment on my compassionate ability to offer comfort to my patients, but was even way more peaked by my life's "genuinely glowing," pre-destined purpose. Yet, "exactly what," he pondered was God calling me to do? It was now that I would answer back about "mindfully channeling this Lord-driven labor" and that especially here in the homestretch, I had a million questions myself. Like, why was the Lord still continuing to have me silently "sit that hot seat" amidst always seeming to fail miserably in the past with any man that I'd loved in my life? After all, I further explained how I'd only be good enough for my changed fiancé's ring when I was considered "financially independent." But, from the moment "it didn't feel right in God's eyes for me to do things this way," he'd forgotten from first grade to share? And, what good was it to keep my focus upon timely completing this tapestry-threaded journey, when he kept his focus on anything but? Though, in this eye-opening moment, I also saw how Allen had been truly avoiding "us" by delving into increased housework (and was now even sneaking into the basement to be able to field more calls). On the flip side, I would be ragged on regularly about my "lack of any surplus money, and if my mobile home had sold yet in an attempt to keep me feeling totally inadequate" because whenever his "wilderness" chose to turn inward, he'd hear how wonderful God was in my life! Here too, I would also share with Lester the incredible love-filled journey I'd traveled while birthing this first treasured book. Especially how the Lord would always "send me 'someone' almost magically with the answers" on any subject I needed help most. Then, at this point this angel's "face lit up" while he began flipping through his book's many chapters. Miraculously, once arriving at the last few of his highlighted pages, he stated "This is just what you need to read because YOU ALREADY KNOW why all this is happening." Now, right before my excited eyes was an illuminating paragraph from Dr. Creflo A. Dollar's *Eight Steps to Create the Life You Want*. And, as I read his soul-touching advice, my homestretch mission's real meaning remarkably fell into place!

WORK IT OUT

"It's not always easy to follow God's instructions. It often requires stepping out in faith without knowing the outcome. It means that you obey God by praying for those who have hurt you. It means forgiving them and speaking well of them. It means waiting on God instead of trying to get back at people. It means doing what God says, no matter what the cost. Having character will challenge your destructive habits and unhealthy decisions. It's up to you to leave these things behind and pursue God like never before, so that you can reach the destination He has for you.

Make the decision today to be a true ambassador for Jesus Christ. When your emotions try to get the best of you, choose to exercise character. Make sure that you don't put anything or anyone else above God. Yield to His instructions, no matter how uncomfortable they might be. Put your feelings aside, and practice doing what's right every day. That's how the character of God will be formed in your life."

What an extremely refreshing thought process to end an AWFUL year! Lastly, as Lester offered me his number for any future clarifications, I wrote it down quickly for the phone book in my purse. Yet, amidst leaning over my desk to see exactly what I'd scribbled, he would next let me know that his name as I had written it somehow wasn't right. Excitedly here, like one more "tapestry-threaded comfort quilt" to ending this spiritual story, he would next need to inform me to "just cross my name out as I told you because all my real friends call me MICHAEL." Wow, what another awesome reminder that I am never too old for a great game of Gotcha-last! Besides, if "my life's story begins at home" then pulleezze let the good stuff start! Then, in my excitement two days later, I decided to openly disregard God's "keep quiet" instructions and take matters into my own hands. Furthermore, on none other than New Year's Eve, I hoped to enlighten a sort of down-in-the-dumps Allen on some of the "doors opening up in my life." Now, I would explain (between my two really busy, holiday-scheduled work shifts) how I'd be needing "some extra hours on the computer over the next three weeks, as I planned to finish up this final round of corrections" so I could begin exploring some publishing options by up-and-coming spring. But, instead of being receptive, I was only growled at for not having this book-writing venture good-to-go some years ago. Though sadly here, what my fiance´ really hadn't remembered, was that my unfolding traumatic abuses were so AWFUL to address at the very time that he (my once "truly handpicked-by-the-Lord angel") had stopped being my own unconditional love. Next, as his reeling anger really stung like a "towel-snap to the back of my head," I could now only hope that God felt as well, that I'd humorously been through enough. As not only did I end up eating my opened-my-big-mouth "Misfit" dinner all alone, Allen gruffly refused to watch movies with me, then played games on his computer straight through 'til two a.m.! Somehow too, I sensed how our "teeter-totter-like existence" could never last with one of us so largely attempting to "lean in" while the other would always leave. And, while I knew it would take more than just riding out all the tides to even begin to reverse this surely "more public than my partner" scenario, we didn't stand a snowball's chance of not capsizing without another all-out miracle, and God's expertise at the helm.

I can do all things through Christ who strengthens me.

Philippians 4:13

"NKJV ™"

My "*Life Is How You Look At It*" Homestretch Part V—

From "Total Loser" to Truly Loved

> For we brought nothing into this world, and it
> is certain we can carry nothing out.
>
> 1 Timothy 6:7
>
> "NKJV ™"

Welcome January 2011! Although my surgery was only a few days away, I decided to write as much as I could in the wee hours and work more positively along with Allen's wish to reorganize our rooms. So, while I sorted and shredded old papers, he painted and purged in the basement. Then, as the boys did a wonderful job compacting our "Christmas corner," we even took time out as a couple to sift through some unlabeled boxes of garland and goodies that if no longer worth keeping, simply bit the dust. Yet, if truth be told, I was tired of forever-hearing how there was "no space to hang my children's photos, that I had too many angels in my collection, and how I really needed to sort through all my clothes and clutter" (all-the-while his stuff just lay wherever it landed!) Here too, while placing several new cans of veggies on the usual pantry shelves down in the basement, I now discarded several old, rusty ones he'd saved since 2006! Meanwhile, amongst Allen's "my belongings are cool and yours breaks the rules 'cause it's my house (and my cars)" line of thinking, it wouldn't be long before God would timely reappear to adjust my regressed attitude by regally "biffing me in the back of the head." And, like before He warned, this was no time to "get real" with my mate's ongoing negativity since picking at me was keeping him busy, both not caring if he was ever attentive and not addressing his own backyard. Likewise, the Lord knew that I too, had an alternate agenda! See, not only was it the halfway-point of my "simply lay-down-your-life and live off the Lord's vine" late last summer decision, it was now also six months to the day of Allen's upcoming birthday lunch. And, more than anything, I want to wrap up one of these newly-published books "in some bow-less looking box" just to be able to see his face, as it was only God's divine intervention that opened all these doors up for me. Also, by His religiously turning this once "total loser" into a TOTALLY USED liaison, I was able to realize this dream!

About the same time, my surgery would go well, though I would find myself very tired. Next, as no stranger to Satan's sabotage, my busy thumbs from typing now developed painful arthritis and throbbed beyond belief. So here, my thoughts foremost turned to getting better first, then finishing up this book. Moreover, as my mind continued to remain fatigued even while attending my follow-up appointments, I fell a few times in the snow. And, if there's one thing I know about doing some unexpected "ice ballet" is that it always comes with both bruising and body aches! Yet, while I had truly put my hoped-for goals primarily out of the picture, I found myself praying more to God. Besides, even though I was not able to release any new thoughts on paper, I was still able to review my old. Awesomely too, I discovered that each and every time I'd encountered stressful situations where I had written words like "as fate would have it", "to my surprise" and "lucky for me"—the Lord's really supportive guidance had been beside me ALL ALONG! Furthermore, I, in my heart knew that if He had come on too strong earlier in my frequent struggles, I too, would've fled as well. Here also, I truly witnessed how God had been busy weaving His own tapestry threads amidst my wisdom-filled writings, to one-day wrap this miracle child up in His dependable "Delight yourself in the Lord . . ." comfort quilt when my world came crashing down! Then, about eight days after this insight I would be awakened again in the night, both freely able to channel my thoughts and aching to get back to church.

On January 16, 2011, my less-than-thrilled chauffeur, Allen, would accompany me to Father Noah's Sunday service as I wasn't feeling totally over the hump yet, and loved having him along. Besides, that morning while I spent time positively praying about possibly joining the gym and enlisting the help of a Life Coach, my cast-less fiancé continued to "eternally ever ruminate" over his spending, his stress and his stuff. Now, as we headed into the church (one of us feeling grateful, while the other grumbling like he'd really rather go for a root canal), I can remember asking several things inquisitively to God. Like, "What good was it doing me to willfully awaken in the night amidst hunkering down in the homestretch to continually walk all alone?" Especially when Allen's overall actions painfully loathed me more than I was passionately loved? So here, while we waited for Father Noah to approach the altar, I realized how truly abandoned I felt. Next, I silently pondered four things I'd long ago written that "popped right into my head." Number one, "When you take others for granted they go" second, "Sometimes the best things in life happen, when we are loneliest and not really looking," and "Just because someone appears unreachable doesn't mean they are unlovable." And, lastly, "If your life's journey is truly NOT sparkling, what aren't you doing about it?" Then, just when I was about to beg God for an instant opt-out to all this insight, Father Noah began to speak. Today, his expressive wisdom and wine for his thirsty audience would be all about "being faith-filled instead of fear-filled," especially at those times when your face really hits the floor. Now, he would question aloud whether any of his parishioners had recently found themselves stuck in such a hurtful and humbling place. Suddenly, as I sat right next to my own once-GRATEFUL hero (who'd also talk kindly to me for hours) my tears began to gush. Though now, as I could easily purge my pent-up grief while within these proven walls, a heightened "sense of peace and purpose" began to invade my fatigued body, while my forlorn heart was instantly surged with that familiar spark of God's so healing light! And, as usual, the warmth of "The Holy Spirit's presence would divinely welcome me as well with such passionate hope and inspiration," an event I'd always experienced just walking through this church's door. At the same time, my partner would begin to painfully whine and wriggle, as he'd caught his thumb between the kneeling cushion and its woodwork when folding it back up into our pew! So next, I'd quietly ponder to God, after being truly exhausted from being "awoken every night amidst always walking on eggshells" and the obvious fact that Allen would rather be anywhere else but with me, "What did I, as this pledged lighthouse of life lessons, have possibly left to portray?" After all, for my financially frazzled fiancé to ever see the light again it would have to drop right on to his head! Meanwhile, I was really tired of not laughing and loving anymore with my once-so-awesome best friend, due to both the ongoing side effects of non-compliance and the AWFUL games going on at home. Besides, for all those times my love would hold me close and tell me tenderly "I'm not going anywhere, Babe," even amidst The Gospel, I felt like he'd already gone.

Meanwhile, I didn't know if I'd even be living in the area once published, as so wanting to follow in Jesus' sometimes "really unpopular footsteps" to light up the lives of others in need. Though, here again God would interject how I was to continue to forge along, both "prayerfully and peacefully" with Allen, without wishing him any paybacks. And, whether we ended up being better friends than fiancé(e)s, I'd best find some amicable faith to proceed. Especially since keeping even the smallest of grudges does not allow the "seeds of our chosen pathway" successfully ever to grow. Then, Father Noah would instruct us to join him in singing only the first two parts of an insightful, "I hadn't-heard-since-a-child-in-church-with-Poppy" so very awakening-with-answers hymn.

Here I Am, Lord

I, the Lord of sea and sky,
I have heard my people cry.
All who dwell in dark and sin
My hand will save.

I, who made the stars of night,
I will make their darkness bright.
Who will bear my light to them?
Whom shall I send?

Here I am, Lord. Is it I, Lord?
I have heard you calling in the night.
I will go Lord, if you lead me.
I will hold your people in my heart.

I, the Lord of snow and rain,
I have borne my people's pain.
I have wept for love of them.
They turn away.

I will break their hearts of stone,
Give them hearts for love alone.
I will speak my word to them.
Whom shall I send?

Here I am, Lord. Is it I, Lord?
I have heard you calling in the night.
I will go Lord, if you lead me.
I will hold your people in my heart.

And, while these illuminating lyrics would help me to understand how when I told God He could "take me however He saw fit to use my pre-destined talents," they were needed most at home. Here too, I learned, that the main reason I was silently sitting in all the "devil's dismal darkness" is because at the end of this fruitful writing journey, it will only be my finally published victory that blissfully "flips" on again the Lord's light switch.

Now, Father Noah would proceed toward wrapping up this service. When suddenly all our usual spiritual normalcy went out the stained glass windows as somehow everything from "the correct order of hymns to our two communion lines" got botched up all at once! And, while each and every one was laughing beyond belief, Allen would next lean over and lovingly whisper "Babe, we've got to join this church!"

It was now the third week of January. Here, I found myself pushing back my anticipated early February deadline by another dreaded week. Likewise, returning to work had become so topsy-turvy, I ended up with several untimely afternoon shifts that didn't allow me to wake up and write. At the same time, that suddenly interested-in-my-mobile-home lady would appear, and need to firm up some loose ends financially, then planned to negotiate a sale by the spring. And, while this delayed action would truly reinforce how a "just let go and let God" knew exactly what He was doing in my life; I couldn't say the same for the struggling man I had at home. Meanwhile, Allen's own challenging "hot seat" had gone from simmer to scalding at the drop of a hat, making his heightened avoidance and hissy fits all the less conducive to my prompt finishing of these pages. Next, within a few days timeframe, he would learn how his company "might need to phase out his health-related department by late next year" if everyone didn't pull together to reduce their existing red. At the same time, his mandatory license for the above occupation arrived in the mail and was set to expire in May. That was, unless a series of online courses and necessary in-services were completed in a timely manner then sent in overnight express to keep his skills up to snuff. Woefully too, as all the repairs around the house seemed to really magnify, my partner's major stress over having to "part with any stored-up savings" turned to serious overload! Yet now, instead of saying much, I'd just lean in and listen. Besides, I'd been really busy also giving away my personal clutter, instituting more financial fix-ups and working foremost on the awesome relationship I cherished most with God. Yet, as the raining chaos in Allen's life would relentlessly continue, those necessary online courses were rescheduled once he'd taken time off from work, his doctor appointments had seemingly multiplied and our snow-dumped Buffalo area's weather was a total detriment to getting things done. Here also, my bewildered fiancé would be pursuing regular updates on where "I stood" with making all this turbulence stop, including both the prompt sale of my mobile home, and this book's onward (so-seemingly at a snail's pace) trek towards publishing success. Therefore next, I would honestly answer Allen that although "my mobile home had sparked some interest," no final offers had come in. Then, I informed him as well how "my editor would be here later in the week to help prepare my manuscript for an up-and-coming submission," magnificently getting me one step closer to my passionate publishing goal. But, foremost, I knew that if I reached out to send "the old Nancy" running to the rescue, I would only be more reamed-out while things were going this wrong.

So, at this point, I surrendered my increasing concerns to God and The Holy Spirit's "however YOU see fit" outcome, then practically had to "do some cartwheels" of my own to even get close to this computer. Besides, between Allen's challenging online re-certification and consistent war games to cope, I knew I couldn't manage without some revitalizing evening naps as well, to keep writing throughout the night. (Where here too, at the height of my humiliation, I unexpectedly discovered that while attempting to comfortably rest upstairs, that I could somehow hear those "sneaky basement conversations" booming from our bedroom's heat vents—causing me next, to seriously lose my appetite and also the urge to cook.) And, as my deadline inched just days away, I was having some real issues too. See, amidst the inclement weather and my reeling work schedules, Father Noah couldn't find time to see me and, although my editor, Phyllis, had returned from vacation, she was very hard to reach.

Moreover, as that insurmountable fear reappeared, likening "the exact computer specs needed toward preparing this book" to the climbing again of Mt. Everest, it would be a very supportive "Renee" at my publishing company who would put my jitters easily at ease. See, positively next, in her encouraging-as-always voice she'd state, "Submitting your manuscript is the most important part, so just get it into my hands." Then, once they'd promptly received it, each awaiting person would pass it along amongst their expertise until all the pieces fell into place. Amazingly here also, upon reviewing some old, printed papers I'd stashed while doing "some earlier writing-based research" (and only a few days after Allen's original "AWFUL birthday outburst"), there contained an ad for publishing Christian books from none other than the above! Now, even as this divine timing was surely winding down, I would find myself praying for "patience, peace and productivity" truly so much more.

Next, God would reappear to insightfully point out how Allen's continued "financial worrywart issues" (as he'd always told me also) were actually some deep-rooted scars from his hurtful past relationships, and the only way I could help to break this process was to compassionately teach him to trust. Besides, between the faithful Lord's teachings and Dave Ramsey's illuminating "money loophole lectures," I was all-out learning too! Surprisingly, I was far from an expert at budgeting and therefore, Allen's so startling-at-times-revelations were seriously right on! Yet now, between all the stress and the struggles, our communication had surely ceased. Though, amongst more baby steps, I'd also gently remind my partner that "years ago when we found ourselves majorly wedged in any tough spots, we took the time out together to meditate and pray." And, that "maybe he was going through all of this genuine upheaval so the Lord might have him 'get real' with his chameleon-like life"—as always needing to be the "eternal hero" for all the work-related chaos and any other's "woe-me" crises, while I was expected to unequally answer for things so trivial as a forgotten-to-re-insert garbage bag the minute he got home. But, here as well, would appear another "in neon lights" Life Lesson as intuitively I knew, I would need to continue to give this "blessed venture" my BEST because no matter what I'd been through God HAD NEVER bailed on me.

My *Life Is How You Look At It* Homestretch Part VI—

From Faith and Fumbles to Figuring It Out

> Therefore humble yourselves under the mighty
> hand of God, that He may exalt you in due time,
>
> 1 Peter 5:6
>
> "NKJV™"

Then unexpectedly, with less than a week to go to send in my manuscript, "the mobile home lady" called also since her plans had hit a glitch. Though, God and I both knew that I had no choice but to patiently wait this one out as these were the necessary funds needed to pay for using "all the other's awesome extras" I'd inserted in my pages; and to excitedly order also my very first round of books. Then incredibly, while truly handing all of this "tornado's likeness" over to the Lord while still obediently keeping my secret, I no longer felt any traces of fear! Because for all those times I had thought I'd need to "enlist the help of a Life Coach," His truly nurturing guidance was just the thing to keep my goals afloat. Besides, sometimes the biggest gifts we are spiritually given are the ones without baubles and bows! But, more than anything, I'd found the more I'd written, I'd risked and risen—allowing me now to set-in-stone believe loving God must come first in my life.

It was now Sunday, February 6, 2011, a few days before this story's expected submission and Allen and I were off to church. Here, Father Noah was full of his usual humor and also heart-wrenchingly serious about other things. Then, he'd make mention of "all the masks we wear in public" yet if we are willing to totally remove them, then real vulnerability is where it's at! Next, my pastor would instruct further that if along our winding paths should we "be TOUCHED IN ANY WAY by God's enlightening wisdom", it is our heavenly obligation to spread these sacred stories in an all-out effort to help jump-start other's healing hearts. Then, when Father Noah insightfully reflected upon why many "once-loving marital relationships turn too early into divorce"—a real lack of communication, amidst an inability to ever apologize, were usually at the root. So, with this enlightening tidbit, I went home hopeful (even though we were not married) that with the help of The Holy Spirit, Allen and I might be able to "somehow awaken that old avenue again." Though, even with me making the first move, the stonewalling priorities of playing on the computer and painting the basement floor took a sad precedence over anything I hoped that we'd say.

Yet, here also, I lovingly remembered from my previously written memoirs how "Although we are ALL survivors of something, life is less about looking backwards and more about learning to heal." Then, from continuing to read *Love & Respect*, I also grasped that many at-odds couples may incredibly find their way back to balanced with only one mate remaining in touch with God. But, I also knew how my many "clustered challenges" had certainly changed me into a blossoming Christian butterfly/beacon that I certainly couldn't cram back! Miraculously too, from regularly reading my Bible, I'd forever learned how as some people spiritually enter our lives for only a reason or a season, I really wouldn't want to have had it any other way. Therefore, while all is ultimately left up to God's timing and this so-illuminating adventure will be submitted before our true relationship's results are known, there was none other than my once tender hearted Allen I would've wanted along for this ride. Though, the hardest part of this "puzzling homestretch's pursuit" is knowing that throughout all the struggles, scrapes and set-backs that we'd experienced (and even amidst the beautiful red roses, chocolates and card I'd excitedly received last Valentine's Day), there may not, at the end-of-this-revealing rainbow's expedition, even be an "us."

Likewise, my step mom, Lucy's, eternal advice of "Be careful what you wish for, Babe," was so much harder to swallow. Especially since I'd asked God to seriously leave no stone unturned, amongst the painful the "Truth will set you free" subject of what was really going on in my life. Yet, while also seeking out the Lord's faithfulness to confront head-on seemingly the makings of my worst nightmare, this testimony shows that even while battling all the hailstorms found in facing any ongoing heartbreak, it was solidly God's Golden Grip that has so surely held me up! Ironically too, while one of us was basically glowing in the dark from his so obvious "ego-boost high" from sneaking around (seemingly) under my radar, the Lord was simultaneously reflecting this bittersweet situation's "ask and you shall receive enlightenment" back, as the ONLY way to end this part.

At this point, I also envisioned clearly how unlike any fairy tale's ending a couple's dreams don't always end up going the way that they had planned. Because sometimes, when *Life Is How YOU Look At It* (even with precious puppies to snuggle), without some dignity "date nights" and a shared, determination to pursue some common interests love is not enough. Next, it would take my penned "Acknowledgements section" to show me how my sacred journey had sweetly come full circle. As here, when I mindfully scanned, "Yet, most important is my gratitude to God for blessing me with true family and tender friendships, amidst teaching me that no matter how AWFUL my life gets, I have the choice to let go with love" I now fully understood! At this point, I also discovered that while others were so busy judging, all I "seemingly wasn't doing without two nickels to rub together" the Lord was jubilantly instilling my ability to remarkably pass along these works. Above all, as that previously envisioned rainbow's newly-found "pot of gold's treasure" reveals—"For all those times when others seem to be treating us primarily as 'crappable', is just the time that Jesus incubates us warmly under his wing and proves that we are CAPABLE!"

Then, positively here, I took from my precious poem that started this whole awakening . . .

There are two choices to live out your days;
Full of regret or afraid to take chances . . .
Or risk yourself fully to find your authentic life,
Based on peace, fearlessness and slow dances.
So when each day dawns I will celebrate,
The gifts of my hero, my angel my pal
Safely resting my head in the fortress of His arms,
Proving God really answers "knee mail."
He is the treasure I won't take for granted,
Knowing together that we'll both grow old
I am now prepared for Him to come,
I've seen the light, freed the doves . . .

FOUND THE GOLD!

Furthermore, to my cherished readers: I hope that my previously written ending to *The Poem That Wouldn't Leave Me Alone* will be as much of a "healing and inspirational heirloom" as it was in helping me. Finally, it is so awesome to know that God's Great Goodness is never all out of miracles! As even now, while "the mobile home lady talks of hiring some movers," you wouldn't be holding these "sow" grateful to be crossing-the-finish-line-pages if I hadn't been totally inspired to "take my own mask fully off to reap the Lord's light" amidst giving ALL the glory to Him!

> It is good for me that I have been afflicted, That I may learn Your statutes. The law of Your mouth is better to me Than thousands of coins of gold and silver.
>
> Psalm 119:71-72
> "NKJV ™"

And, may you tirelessly find the courage also, to trust in your true purpose!

In Peace and Prayers . . .

Love, Nancy

But now, O LORD,
You are our Father;
We are the clay, and You our potter;
And all we are the work of Your hand.

Isaiah 64:8

"NKJV™"

The "Special Three" Who Were Meant to Be

With love and thanks to three very special people who, along with God in my sacred journey of achieving "the seemingly insurmountable," never-gave-up-hope on this single mom! To my little brother Chris and Mr. Shelby Kennedy of Tennessee, who've both been blessed and truly "comfort-quilt connected to me" amidst the treasured talents of Reba McEntire, you two were always my "shining stars in spirit." Especially, while I've endured the Lord's uncomfortable-at-times testing of this "chosen one's" ability amidst His "you'll need-to-silently take-the-High-Road endeavor," while humbly never forgetting also in my big sister Jerri's memory, how: "There's a little Misfit in each of us just waiting to be held, hugged or heard." Then, amongst the Lord's insightful "What's 'My Word' really worth to you?" challenge, I answered Him back with hefty reductions in my many distractions minus carrying some others' "crusade-hindering baggage" to successfully reach as we all have now, that ULTIMATE crack in the clouds!

Lastly, it is with much gratitude to my editor, Phyllis, that I save my most touching life lesson for here. As most recently while we sat one summer evening on my front porch with "our eyes all bloodshot from super-screening this work," I saw very clearly amidst this book's both pruning and productive process, that God had gratefully bestowed upon me yet again another priceless gift! While I already knew that both Poppy and my "big sister, Jerri," would certainly be causing major hoopla up in Heaven at the almost publishing of my passion, the Lord had also paved the way, as well, with "another angel on my wavelength" by providing me with Phyllis. And, by simply borrowing someone else's sweet big sister, who'd also been-there-done-that published, we were proudly able to see this "from victim to Victorious" pact we shared, fruitfully all the way through. (While also exhibiting wonderfully as well, how those who've truly reached their peak in life must remember to always "reach back!")

Yet, this effort did not come without some real hitches and glitches as we finally explored these evolving (yet unedited) pages from over the last three weeks. On this night, I would also vulnerably share with Phyllis how I truly "would not have made it financially another week on paper" if God had not so solidly kept His promise and my mobile home hadn't sold when it did. Then, she would chime in next with her parakeet-on-a-pedestal take that: "What kept her most hungry" for doing more of her after-hours editing was how I had (seemingly) trumped while armed only with God's Biblical road map right over my tapestry threads of abuse. Though now, I'd have to remind Phyllis amongst our heartfelt night's discussion how things aren't always what they seem. After all, the more I was making strides in my enlightening expedition to "willfully scale Mt. Everest," the more I was encountering (as obviously Satan's most boisterous attempt to sabotage this sacred mission), several blatantly angry and abusive behind-the-scenes people in ALL my walks of life. This scenario had especially rung true over the last six weeks when it was assumed all right for me to be treated "as both invisible and inconvenient, while still working inconspicuously beneath the Lord's truly comforting camouflage"—until someone else's really pressure-filled life would overwhelmingly overflow. Then, I was expected to trade in this (while unbeknownst-to-most) miraculously manifested "third job," to do more cartwheels and clean up THEIR mess. Yet, positively too, the more the devil was trying to "ping me," God was parting the Red Sea! Like the day when this entire manuscript somehow deleted unexpectedly from the computer, the Lord promptly saw to it, that I'd get my book back. And, those recent permission requests I'd sent out as required to use "some of the other author's excerpts" (after applying extra elbow grease and pursuing many dead-end phone calls) would be returned to me expressly in days instead of weeks!

But, more than anything, I next told Phyllis how I felt most recently, like my life was suddenly being forced to somehow fit (like a terribly squished orange!) into the "top part of a triangle." And, while I didn't fully understand this divine action's meaning, there was one thing I knew for sure! As foremost, with God's eyes now ALWAYS lovingly upon me and while finally fixin' to publish, I was unable to persistently fix any other's "drama-filled challenges," but could always PRAY they'd find their way! Besides, the further up this desolate mountain I headed while being accompanied only by the Lord's "I am your rock" promise, the more I carefully protected my downtime and pursued peace in my changing life. I even awoke earlier to study more of my Bible's blessed armor, and began to regularly walk again the energizing rainbow-filled wonder of Niagara Falls' majestic mist. To my delight also, how different my daily "to-do list" flowed when

I made time to start off on the right foot and put praising God's revelations first.

Though lastly, during Phyllis' and my very first porch picnic-discussion, I would ponder one looming thought out loud, as our "life lessons" always are the hardest when it's US who has to live them. As somehow, since I'd only recently returned with family from visiting others we loved in Rochester (and after simply chalking up some unforeseen car troubles and another's chronic crankiness), there was one crushing situation I'd encountered that was still somehow stuck in my craw. After all, as Phyllis next shared with me how she "would soon be turning 50," this younger sister was struggling so-orphaned-like more with something I'd read while I was away. You see, during the last weekend, I had been taking the time to foremost check out some other authors' "final section formats" when I'd suddenly endure something so heart-wrenchingly painful, it even turned off my gift to write! Sadly here, one accomplished writer's insightful finale included the thanking of those cherished members (in my words) "that were amidst her closest circle" for always ensuring that she had peaceful surroundings and prayer-filled backings as she completed her God-given goal. Where suddenly, it was mirrored as well, that the same magnificent Lord who'd brought us together would be the main subject to rip us apart.

Then finally, I told my own awesome editor how I'd uniquely gone from not only being "a once timid bird on the balcony who always walked on eggshells," to steadfastly, one-foot-in-front-of-the-other conquering my fear of flying solo while now always well within God's reach. Though, here also, I was only getting "some sporadic, angry phone calls at my desk" to harshly point out with ruffled feathers all I wasn't perfectly accomplishing at home. Yet, that's right when I insightfully saw again that Almighty God knew just exactly what wisdom to "send my way through someone," to wondrously stop anyone else's doubts and digs from weighing down my wings! As in the end, I'm living proof that it is possible to experience the ultimate of victory in an unbelieving valley, since my editor would next invaluably (and off the top of her head!) reveal, "The reason you feel so defeated-at-times Nancy, is because . . .

"It's so much easier for them to drag you down, than it is to LIFT them up."

~Phyllis Stallard

A Word to Readers

Trust in the Lord with all your heart, And lean not on your own understanding; In all your ways acknowledge Him, And He shall direct your paths.

Proverbs 3:5-6

NKJV™

Sweetly, one of the things that stands out most to me as this book comes to a close is from my "What Are You Willing To Give Up To Achieve Your Dream's?" questions. As I know, from "pre-destined to perseverance," good things WILL always come to those who wait and God's Love WILL always provide! Though at this point too, I'd again live and learn, how sometimes while I'm so busy pestering God for some "please, get me off this hot seat 'STAT' answers" (instead of just humbly paying attention!), He humorously puts them right under my nose. After all, it was the Lord who had told me about two weeks earlier how I'd "better buckle down and finish reading another one of Joyce Meyer's books" in time to loan it as weeks-earlier promised to Phyllis. But, willfully here, I chose instead to disregard His eternal expertise and then (unnaturally-for-me now) began to "question, quease and quiver" over the unexplained reason for my newest barrage of those intuitive bells and whistles. Moreover, I'd also been distracted with searching up-and-down, as well, for the most perfect of mind-blowing wisdom be it in poems, prayers or paperbacks to properly end this book. So, on the very afternoon that I knew that Phyllis was coming, I traded in my breaks at work to push past my procrastination and timely read the last few pages of Joyce's "NEVER GIVE UP!" pronto—from the sweltering heat in my car, only once I pulled it out of my trunk! Then, at this moment, the real explanation for my frequent rash of uphill battles amid giving funds and freebies away to others was explained before my weary "sparrow on a streetlight eyes" in her been-there-done-that words:

"When we decide to walk that narrow path, God begins requiring more of us. He starts taking away some of our fleshly baggage. He pulls the padding out of our nest. He asks us to let go of some of our old ways, to adjust some of our attitudes, to raise the standards in our relationships and conversations, and to make some changes in the ways we spend our time and money.

Everything God asks us to do as we walk the narrow way may not be easy, but it will be good for us. It may not feel like a blessing as we got through it, but it leads to blessing in the end. It will require us to overcome some things, but it will lead us to wonderful rewards.

I encourage you to get on the narrow road and stay there. There may not be many people on it with you, but if you look carefully you will see Jesus because the narrow way is always the road He travels. Do not go back to the broad road when the narrow one loses its appeal. The broad road is deceptive. It may be fun for a while, it may be easy, but it leads to trouble. Pay the price to stay with God on the road that leads to life."

~ Joyce Meyer

Though in the end, God would not be the (*Life Is How YOU Look At It*, Missy!) Lord, I've so grown to love—without getting the very last laugh! After all, if I'd only read the above paragraphs two weeks earlier as instructed, I would have known on this "very last mile of my Mt. Everest mission" exactly what it all meant! Moreover, Father Noah's special sermon was seriously "right on" too, because if we dare to just bravely Leap before we Look; God "does faithfully stand behind us after the fact to see our journey bear sweet fruit."

"I am the vine, you are the branches. He who abides in Me, and I in him, bears much fruit; for without Me you can do nothing.

John 15:5

"NKJV ™"

My Hardest Life Lesson For Last

"Peace I leave with you, My peace I give to you; not as the world gives do I give to you. Let not your heart be troubled, neither let it be afraid.

John 14:27

"NKJV ™"

While there may have been days in everyone's past when we were the "total decoy" used by the devil, the reality remains now in neon lights it was up to US to walk away. Meanwhile too, while I'd been busy being respectful to my fiancé over these roller-coaster months (and still addressing my own many faults!), our climate had certainly changed. We were actually learning to "talk, take walks and make eye contact again" while the Lord fully worked on me to forge through the pain of all those "fizzled birthdays, secretive phone calls and forgotten anniversaries;" and shifted my thoughts instead to the fact that FORGIVENESS FELT REALLY GOOD! But, it would be here at this point also that my *Life Is How YOU*

*Look At It*s unique mission would be put to the ultimate test! As it seems, Mother Nature had another "huge storm brewing on our couple's horizon," to see exactly how we'd both handle it and where we each would turn to cope. Yet, at this time too, I was busy reading some really good books, listening to Christian radio for right-what I-needed guidance and seeking out insight from my church-going friends who also became my trusty "ravens-on-the-rock" as I finished up this trek.

Though, my previous "personal tsunami" would pale in comparison to the slowly leaking can of chaos that would suddenly come to light next. Likewise, it had been God who'd spent these past sixteen months showing me tirelessly how if I would continue to put in all the "elbow grease needed for this spiritual mission," that He'd provide the icing on the cake! Meanwhile, this thought also allowed me to recall here-and-now (as once only over that blessed rainbow!) a blazing outburst that I had forgot happened between "Allen" and me right before we'd planned to wed. See, on that confusing day, amidst his face being all contorted, he was expressing his anger this time at the fact, that I'd honestly told a family member a few months earlier that "if I was ever to get married again it would only be to a Christian man." And, while this from-the-heart remark really seemed to "rock the world" I so believed that we were based on, I had a hard time understanding why. As in retrospect, the Lord knew exactly what He was doing by keeping me willfully "humbled and humiliated" instead of ("Why not God?") on our honeymoon. Since incredibly, only after becoming an "enlightened eagle on His embankment," I suddenly saw how our real issue wasn't all about my "lousy bank account balance" or "inability to be the perfect maid." But, that even around the time of our latest cherished Vermont trip, those expert meddlers and other energy-zapping "priorities" that were so corrosive to our couple's pyramid allowably kept strife smoldering behind the scenes! Moreover, while no way to ever truly sanctify a marriage as the Lord would next unveil, the real fact remained, that even amongst my "growing laundry list of inadequacies," I just wasn't (amid finally confronting with God's help, Allen's "outside-of-us behavior") ever upheld like them.

> So husbands ought to love their own wives as
> their own bodies; he who loves his wife loves himself.
> For no one ever hated his own flesh, but nourishes
> and cherishes it, just as the Lord does the church.
> Ephesians 5:28-29
> "NKJV ™"

Though, the Lord was foremost teaching me here to honor His "love unconditionally at-all-costs principles," even though

I felt like I wanted to scream! But, most supremely, I'd found from studying my Bible that if Jesus "could lay down His life for our sins" then I could endure such uphill too! Besides, the more I chose to FAST instead of eating throughout this "What's the blessing in this avalanche's Lord, really raw rejection?" the more I benefited two-fold. With more free flowing energy I could easily hear God's really "parental-at-times" lectures, and was putting a prayer-assisted dent also into losing that last twenty pounds. At the same time I was completing these final pages, that "carwash of chaos" resurged tenfold—from distancing, to dog costs to dental work. While next, Allen's so-glowing "pals, paychecks and put-downs" unfolded again, amongst his surviving a major layoff; making me feel more like I existed with a (supposed) Solitaire-playing stranger, at the time when I needed him most. But, things were very different now. If truth be told, after just finishing up my pledge to live off God's vine for a year, I'd blissfully learned to be less affected by anyone's "condescending-to-my-spirit treatment" and more energized completely by God's trustworthy sap!

Yet, I really wasn't kidding when I'd previously mentioned how the Lord had been busy saving my so-purposely avoided, but from-the-heart written "Sometimes the best things in life happen, when we are loneliest and not really looking" hardest life lesson for last. As above all, I knew, while heading closer to that top of the triangle, the time was inching closer as well, to finally confronting (amidst all the religion-based "ripples in our relationship") that pink elephant in the room. Because sometimes, if *Life Is How You Look At It* when a Born-again butterfly tries to spread her wings, her other half stays behind. Here also, I would learn, that, "wishing and hoping won't change people" only the Lord's Word changes people, as my own cherished walk became less about defending my "boringness" and more about deepening my bond with Him! Positively too, even as Allen has just returned from a weekend trip with a new, purple-boxed Bible stuffed (Woo-hoo) within his suitcase—I knew, I'd go again through all the growing pains and partner-wasn't-proud landslides I've weathered, to know who I am today.

So, in the end, while I want nothing more than to see Allen end up happy, I've found (even as I continue to make some final changes on that "divine" home computer), he'll need to solely "keep speeding up the hamster wheel" of his already million work shifts while I wait calmly for God's green light. As to ever complete our cherished callings we CANNOT do it alone.

> And we know that all things work together for good to those who love God, to those who are the called according to His purpose.
>
> Romans 8:28
> "NKJV™"

Though, foremost I sensed that "due to both my obvious and ongoing disobedience to His word," God was no longer willing to "encourage further works" or would be able to send my way a new, more-balanced relationship, from a roost where I had too, at times lost my focus and I no longer thrived.

Then, shockingly too, "Hurricane Irene" began to wreak havoc upon the Northeast, sending my oldest daughter not only scrambling home ill from New York City; but my much-needed "quote usage request" for this very piece would become somewhat delayed as well. Also, as a result of this storm's erratic path, that very special-to-us state of Vermont became so post-storm flooded, that people were stranded all over the place. All this, while really successfully trying to sparkle amongst suddenly being enlightened as well, in the so-humorous words of one of Father Noah's surely silliest sermons ever, how it's "hardest to prevail in any sacred endeavor" while heart wrenchingly and repeatedly only being told how much "you stink." (Also, dear readers, "if you were to die tomorrow where does the Lord's Place stand today?" Did your spouse even make your agenda, or were they only kept around in the once so-awesome picture to be your premier "house hag" or primary health insurance?)

Next, while meditating with God one September 2011 night, after feeling like some others' "seriously mean-spirited straws" had surely broken this car chooser's back, I asked Him what I should expect next. That's right, when He blitzed back straight to my soul (sweetly bypassing as well, my heaped-on shame and sorrow), the determined words; "Ninety Days to a New Life." Likewise, my thirtieth class reunion had gone wonderful weeks-earlier, and as my abundant blessings continued to blossom with every single challenge, Beth would also be finishing up Grad School by later in the spring!

Meanwhile, at the very last of Father Noah's sermons that Allen and I would attend together, our Reverend was making mention of others' inquisitive reactions to us living near Niagara Falls. At the same time, he would ask us worshippers "if we'd be willing to do WHATEVER effort it took" to get our God-given talents off the ground before they forever-withered away. Even if it meant (hypothetically) "jumping over Niagara Falls without a barrel while truly knowing the Lord would be there?" Lastly, would we totally risk some people's "painful persecution and all those things we know as normal" to launch His purposeful life? And, even after enduring my own two jobs' ongoing cuts and many months of being harshly ostracized elsewhere, as I blindly pursued my passion; I not only knew my biggest test had arrived, but what my "ask BOLDLY" answer must be! As along these lines "living Christian" isn't a long term cure-all, but a treasured lifestyle choice. Where wondrously too, I'm looking forward to the day my Trusty Savior will send my way His chosen "special hand-picked someone" among more "love can move mountains!" insights to be each other's safe haven in any storms.

Though happily here, in tribute to one of my very special "Michael's" (Michael Jordan), I can think of no better thought than yours to proudly end this piece. As it seems that you just always kept on asking me amid my ongoing brokenness, "After being there for everyone else each day, when you get home WHO holds you?" Where naturally, this point-blank question made me very uncomfortable over the years, because I never had a vibrant comeback, or a solid relationship based on trust. Yet, once finding out WHO really does after seeing faith-first how it is impossible to be "both scuffed around under-the-world's shoes" and shine brightly as His beacon as well, I finally have your hands-down answer. As now, after "wholeheartedly" surviving this journey's GRATEFULLY asked-for hindsight, amidst His divinely disclosed revelations (while also hearing here-and-there woefully, throughout the years "Don't let the door hit you . . .")—God did, God does and He ALWAYS DELIVERS even when our world's upside down! But, more than anything, His all-out miracles happen most to those who'll just purge their million priorities and passionately JUST BELIEVE!

"For everyone who asks receives, and he who seeks finds, and to him who knocks it will be opened.

Luke 11:10

"NKJV ™"

Finally, amidst all the deafening silence and deterring heartache at home," I asked the Lord to please show me why I was even still here. Especially, since I felt, like every inch of my being, had amongst such a family "heave-ho"—truly exhausted all my options and had nothing left to give? Yet, as I began the illuminating ritual of praying without ceasing, the Biblical passage for which I had been digging in regards to, "Did I successfully manage to share my 'sacred gift of light' in such a dismal environment?" would suddenly as God had promised, "ALL make sense, Missy" in the end . . .

And seeing the multitudes, He went up on a mountain, and when He was seated His disciples came to Him. Then He opened His mouth and taught them, saying:

"Blessed are the poor in spirit,
    For theirs is the kingdom of heaven.
Blessed are those who mourn,
    For they shall be comforted.
Blessed are the meek,
    For they shall inherit the earth.

Blessed are those who hunger and thirst for
righteousness,
For they shall be filled.
Blessed are the merciful,
For they shall obtain mercy.
Blessed are the pure in heart,
For they shall see God.
Blessed are the peacemakers,
For they shall be called sons of God.
Blessed are those who are persecuted for
righteousness' sake,
For theirs is the kingdom of heaven.

"You are the light of the world. A city that is set on a hill cannot be hidden. "Nor do they light a lamp and put it under a basket, but on a lampstand, and it gives light to all who are in the house. "Let your light so shine before men, that they may see your good works and glorify your Father in heaven.

Matthew 5: 1-10, 14-16

"NKJV™"

See, for all those times that I was "ignored and treated unworthy" because God's timing was misunderstood, He'd used my own "gifted light" to repel such negativity, and turned real darkness into good!

"Has God spoken a word to your heart? Has He given you a dream or vision that has not yet come to fruition? He may have told you something awesome that you are going to do for His Kingdom; something that will propel you into a life of overflowing abundance, and it looks like the odds are against you. Don't be discouraged. If you can see it by faith, you CAN have it.

Many people get caught up in what THEY want to do instead of finding out what God wants them to do. That's why people waste years pursuing endeavors God hasn't called them to undertake, and then get frustrated and blame Him when things don't work out. However, they didn't seek God's wisdom on what they were trying to do! Before stepping out, seek God first. That demonstrates your first priority—fulfilling God's will, not your own.

There is a time and a season for every purpose (Ecclesiastes 3:1). God has developed the master plan for your life, and He knows exactly when you and your purpose need to show up. He is all about reaching people and when you achieve your destiny, the people God has called you to reach will be impacted forever."

Dr. Creflo A. Dollar

(From 8 STEPS TO CREATE THE LIFE YOU WANT by Dr. Creflo A. Dollar. Copyright © 2008 by Dr. Creflo A. Dollar.
By permission of Faith Words)

Commit your works to the Lord, And your thoughts will be established. A man's heart plans his way, But the Lord directs his steps.

Proverbs 16: 3, 9.

"NKJV ™"

About the Author

Not that I speak in regard to need, for I have
learned in whatever state I am, to be content:

Philippians 4:11

"NKJV ™"

Nancy Loss lives in the Western New York area and has been very busy both living off the Lord's vine, and letting Him take the lead. Sweetly too, after "successfully scaling Mt. Everest" she finds herself primarily indebted to God for His illuminating discernment—and is looking forward to becoming a grandmother down the road, spending precious time again with friends and family, and completing with passion and patience her next round of beckoning books.

Moreover, Nancy remains truly grateful for all of her "spiritually-sent" Life Lessons, as she never would have (from darkness-to-dawn) discovered how AWESOMELY God was blessing her life! Also by finding time to foremost "pray, play and celebrate each day," she knows God's faithful parachute will always open if she always focuses upon Him first!

Miraculously too, once ascending upon the "highest peak of Mt. Everest" by finally fixin' to publish, Nancy would see very concretely now, amidst all those "so really rare cracks in the clouds," that it takes more than just commitment, courtesy and a conscience, to ace any loving relationship. As optimally, amongst all the many trials, triumphs and temptations encountered, a couple's "make-it-or-break-it compass must be eternally Christ-centered" to ever sail off into the sunset and live wholesomely ever after.

But Jesus looked at them and said to them, "With men this is impossible, but with God all things are possible."

Matthew 19:26
"NKJV ™"

Notes and Nuggets

***Larger Quotes

Lynne D. Finney, *Reach for the Rainbow: Advanced Healing for Survivors of Sexual Abuse*, A Perigee Book, Published by The Berkley Publishing Group, a division of Penguin Putnam Inc. Copyright © 1990, 1992 by Lynne D. Finney— Cover illustration © by Judy Taylor. Used by permission.

Joyce Meyer, *Life Without Strife* (Lake Mary, FL: Charisma House, 1995, 2000), Used by permission.

Dr. Creflo A. Dollar, 8 Steps to Create the Life You Want. Published by Faith Words, a division of Hachette Book Group, Inc. Copyright © 2008. Used by permission.

Joyce Meyer, NEVER GIVE UP! Published by Faith Words, a division of Hachette Book Group Inc. Copyright © 2008 by Joyce Meyer. Used by permission.

Doreen Virtue, Ph.D. *Divine Prescriptions,*
Published by Renaissance Books,
5858 Wilshire Blvd., Suite 200 Los Angeles California 90036.
Distributed by
St. Martin's Press, Copyright © 2000 by Doreen Virtue, Ph.D.
Used by permission.

***Smaller Notes

Sketches "Missy" Poem (First Chapter)—Written by Ben
Burroughs.

Dr. Joyce Brothers, *How to Get Whatever You Want Out of
Life,* Published by Ballantine Books, a division of Random
House, Inc. By arrangement with Simon & Schuster New York.
Copyright © 1978.

Helen Keller's Inspirational Quotes—taken from:
Helen Keller's Journal 1936-37, Doubleday, Doran & Co.
Garden City, New York 1938,
My Religion, by Helen Keller, Doubleday, Page & Company
Garden City, New York 1927—
And finally, from *Optimism, An Essay*—Published by
T.Y. Crowell and Company 1903